PENGUIN CLASSICS

THE CID/CINNA/THE THEATRICAL ILLUSION

PIERRE CORNEILLE, the French dramatist, was born in Rouen in 1606. After a Jesuit education he worked as Crown Counsel in Rouen, and for many years kept playwriting as his leisure activity. He wrote tragedies and comedies, and his first success came in 1636 with *Le Cid*, a tragi-comedy which made Corneille's reputation as a master of serious drama and established the genre known as French classical tragedy. During the next forty years Corneille produced over twenty-five plays. He died in 1684.

•

JOHN CAIRNCROSS was educated at Glasgow University, at the Sorbonne, and at Trinity College, Cambridge. After a period in the British Civil Service, he settled in Rome, but worked for a time as Chief Editor in the United Nations (ESCSP) in Bangkok. Later, he was Head of the Department of Romance Languages at Western Reserve University, Cleveland. He afterwards moved to the Food and Agricultural Organization of the United Nations (FAO) in Rome. He has translated six of Racine's tragedies in two volumes, *Phaedra and Other Plays* and *Andromache and Other Plays*, and Corneille's *Polyeuctus*, *The Liar* and *Nicomedes* for Penguin Classics, as well as La Fontaine's *Fables* (a selection) and other poems. He is also the author of *Molière bourgeois et libertin*, *After Polygamy was Made a Sin* and *L'humanité de Molière*.

Pierre Corneille

THE CID

CINNA

THE THEATRICAL ILLUSION

Translated and introduced by

JOHN CAIRNCROSS

PENGUIN BOOKS

PENGUIN BOOKS

Published by the Penguin Group
Penguin Books Ltd, 27 Wrights Lane, London W8 5TZ, England
Penguin Books USA Inc., 375 Hudson Street, New York, New York 10014, USA
Penguin Books Australia Ltd, Ringwood, Victoria, Australia
Penguin Books Canada Ltd, 10 Alcorn Avenue, Toronto, Ontario, Canada M4V 3B2
Penguin Books (NZ) Ltd, 182–190 Wairau Road, Auckland 10, New Zealand

Penguin Books Ltd, Registered Offices: Harmondsworth, Middlesex, England

This translation first published 1975
9 10

Printed in England by Clays Ltd, St Ives plc
Set in Monotype Garamond

To K.

CONTENTS

TRANSLATOR'S FOREWORD

WHEN, before his untimely death, my friend Robert Baldick asked me to translate a selection of Corneille's works, I accepted the request with considerable hesitation. I felt that the great French writer's robust and often involved oratorical style presented a much greater challenge than the lucid and lyrical half-tones of Racine, however difficult it may have been to render his subtle and exquisite music in English. And so it proved!

As the three plays for the present volume I chose *The Cid*, which is both a classic and a magnificently stirring drama, *Cinna*, as being representative of Corneille's political (and more specifically Roman) works, and finally *The Theatrical Illusion*, a rather unusual comedy from the period of his early glory. The first two plays raised the most formidable difficulties. I rapidly discovered that nothing was easier than to produce a version which would strike our irreverent age as an uproariously comic caricature. It was essential, therefore, to elaborate a style which would render, at least to some extent, the sustained 'nobility' of Corneille's world. Moreover, for both *Cinna* and *The Theatrical Illusion* there was no alternative to occasional condensation if a line-by-line version was to be achieved in blank verse (which meant sacrificing two syllables in every Alexandrine).

In the end, I found what appeared to me to be a suitable medium which leant heavily on Shakespeare's dramas. My version of *The Cid* satisfied me most, no doubt because of the constant excitement and tension created through the play. *Cinna*, from which this martial glamour is absent, was a much tougher proposition. And for both *Cinna* and *The Theatrical Illusion* the more involved passages have been streamlined. However, the latter play left some latitude, since the comic effects depend on the sense rather than on the style. The intention of the translator was that Corneille should appear clearer, sharper and more terse in English in these two plays than he really is. The present version is probably about as accessible to a modern English reader as the French original was to a contemporary of the author's.

However, what has been attempted is a translation, not an adaptation, and the metre is blank verse and not the misleadingly Restoration rhymed couplets. It is hoped therefore that, despite the occasional stylistic compression, the present versions have preserved the spirit of Corneille.

Rome, March 1973 John Cairncross

PIERRE CORNEILLE

FATE has dealt unkindly with the great seventeenth-century French dramatist, Pierre Corneille, even in his native land. 'As a result of an over-simple and restrictive tradition,' writes Raymond Picard in his admirable analysis of the writer,[1] 'it has long been contended that, of all Corneille's plays, only a handful of tragedies such as *Le Cid*, *Horace*, *Cinna*, or *Pompée* (1637–43) deserve to survive. By disregarding all the rest, critics have had no trouble in reducing Corneille's genius to a few dramatic devices, some psychological stances and a certain lofty tone, and thus, by an obvious over-simplification, they have frozen the founder of the classical theatre in a pose of exaggerated sublimity.' But in fact 'his thirty-two plays show a prodigious range of talent. Far from having worked to a formula, Corneille again and again struck out in original directions, renewing his strength and genius over forty long years of writing. His work pulsates with an extraordinary creative vitality. A tragedy follows a comedy or a tragicomedy; a tragedy-ballet comes after a heroic comedy; and within the same genre there are profound differences between the plays.'

His first plays are poles apart from the stereotype of the bombastic tragedies he is represented as having written. 'With such works as *Mélite*, *La Galerie du Palais* and *La Place Royale* (1629–34), he created an original type of five-act comedy in verse.' They are remarkable for 'the naturalness, the freshness and the grace of the young people [portrayed], the badinage and the wit, the truth to life of the attitudes, the penetrating observation of the manners of the age – all in a simple colloquial style'. As Corneille himself pointed out (in 1634), 'My vein ... often combines the lofty buskin with the comic sock, and ... pleases the audience by striking contrasting notes.'

1. *Two Centuries of French Literature*, pp. 66–82.

'But, at about the same time as Corneille wrote these three "contemporary" comedies, he produced in *Clitandre* an Elizabethan play in which fantasy runs wild. The stage changes from a wood to a prison, and then to a cave. Before the spectator's eyes, Pymantes tries to rape Dorisa who in her turn puts out one of his eyes. Frenzied, utterly impossible actions are enacted in an entirely fanciful world.' *The Theatrical Illusion* (*L'Illusion Comique*), dated 1636, also takes place in this world of fantasy, as readers will see from the Preface and translation of the play in the present volume; the irrepressible Corneille even parodies the martial sentiments of *The Cid* before that play was written.

What is more, though he 'appealed much more to the mind than to the eye in four or five of the finest tragedies of the seventeenth century, ... he continued to delight and astonish visually ... "My main aim," he wrote of the musical play of *Andromède*, "has been to satisfy the visual sense by the gorgeousness and the variety of the scenery and not to appeal to the intellect by cogent arguments or to touch the heart by delicate representations of the passions."'

The second obstacle to Corneille's demummification is the old but tenacious fallacy that his plays represent a school-book conflict, especially in *The Cid*, between 'love which is alleged to be a passion replete with weaknesses and honour which dictates duty. The carefully pondered love, which one feels for and claims from someone whom one deems worthy of it, is also a duty. Rodrigo goes so far as to affirm in a lyrical meditation at the end of the first act

> Duty's not only to my mistress. It
> Is also to my father.[1]

Moreover, the two types of duty do not really conflict. If he does not avenge the insult done to his father, Rodrigo will draw down on himself the contempt of Ximena and will thereby forfeit her love for him, for that love implies esteem and even admiration. Paradoxically it is his love for her, as

1. The equivalent line in this Penguin translation runs:
My duty's to my father, not to her.

well as his honour, that forces him to kill his sweetheart's father and thus to raise an obstacle between the two lovers which might to some appear insurmountable. As soon as Rodrigo has transcended the basic option between cowardice which would have involved the loss of everything – honour and love – and heroism, which is his vocation, he has no alternative but to fulfil his destiny as a hero. In this as in other tragedies, what is *cornélien* is the intolerable and sometimes agonizing situation in which the character is trapped and from which he can free himself only by shouldering his responsibility as a hero.

'Now, as it happens, Corneille's characters are nothing if not heroes. Rodrigo, Horace, Augustus and Nicomedes are of more than human stature. Endowed with extraordinary moral strength, they possess to the utmost degree the virtue of *générosité* (nobility of soul); they are ready to devote all their inner resources to the task of incarnating their sublime image of themselves. Will-power, self-control, courage and judgement, all these enhance man's powers and his greatness. In the humanist world in which they live, it would seem that nothing – misfortune, suffering or catastrophe – can undermine their overweening integrity. Fortified by their energy and stoicism, they have nothing to fear at the hands of Destiny. They will parry its blows, or bear them uncomplainingly. Fate may dog their steps. For them, it is nothing but a congeries of external accidents and mishaps, and it is powerless to force an entry into their hearts and alter their resolve. Man is entirely free and fully responsible. He has no grounds for dreading the gods. When treating the most sombre theme in Greek tragedy, Corneille in his *Oedipe* (1659) radically transforms the spirit of the legend and does not shrink from writing

> The heavens, fair in reward and punishment,
> To give to deeds their penalty or meed
> Must offer us their aid, then let us act.

This concept of free will is clearly borrowed from the Jesuits and the humanist tradition. The tragic element in Corneille, then, is not to be sought in the pathetic helplessness of the characters but in the harrowing circumstances in which a wicked fate has placed them. What we have, in a way, is a tragedy of circumstances, over which the hero must rise superior, relying on his own forces.

'But he does so only after exacting and grievous efforts. Corneille's characters are no cardboard supermen. For them, heroism is not a second nature to which they need merely abandon themselves. They are not sublime automata. They know what suffering is, and they sometimes vent their feelings in lyrical stanzas and in monologues. They are tugged this way and that. They are rent by inner conflicts, and they admit as much. Ximena confesses that Rodrigo "tears [her] heart to pieces"; but she adds, it is "without dividing [her] soul" (III, 3); Pauline also, in *Polyeucte*, recognizes that her duty "tears her soul" although it "does not alter its resolve" (II, 2). There is no doubt that we must jettison the half-baked concept of the swashbuckling Cornelian hero, always sure of himself and unhesitatingly sublime, whose greatness is manifested primarily in a swaggering boastfulness. Even Augustus (in *Cinna*) complains of having "a wavering heart" (IV, 3). It is only at the end of the play when he proves victorious over himself that he exclaims (and this is more wishful thinking than actual fact):

I'm master of myself as of the world. (V, 3)

There is a quivering sensitivity at loggerheads with itself, a three-dimensional reality, in these characters who are too readily described as being all of a piece. Heroism is not something already conferred on them. It is conquered stage by stage as the action unfolds. The hero takes shape before the spectator's eyes. People are not born heroes, they become heroes. Corneille's Theatre is, in the literal sense of the phrase, "a school of moral greatness".

'This greatness is not always synonymous with goodness and virtue. A great crime is also a great deed. Moral power and energy are important in their own right and not only because of the enterprises on which they are brought to bear.

Thus, Cleopatra's crimes in *Rodogune* (1644) "are accompanied by a moral greatness which has something so grandiose about it," notes Corneille, "that, at the same time as we detest her actions, we admire the source from which they spring" (*First Discourse*). What one has to do is to arouse in the spectators' hearts a feeling of astonishment, indeed a transport, whether of horror or admiration, at the deeds of which man is capable at the summit of his powers. Now in Corneille the hero arrives at this paroxysm only when the society in which he lives and his place in it are challenged, when his *gloire* – that is, his dignity, his reputation, his honour – are at stake, as well as the safety of the state. Political interests are regarded as providing the hero with the best opportunity and means for their fulfilment. Hence their important role in this theatre. Love, as against this, remains in the background, for tragedy "calls for some great issue of state . . . and seeks to arouse fears for setbacks which are more serious than the loss of one's mistress". In *Sertorius* (1662), one character asks

> When plans of such importance are conceived,
> Can one put in the balance thoughts of love? (I, 3)

And in the same play, another character gives the following advice:

> Let us, my lord, let's leave for petty souls
> This lowly give and take of amorous sighs. (I, 3)

Love, which is convincingly portrayed in many guises in such a host of characters, may prove their downfall. It cannot shape their destiny.'

It could be added – and the point is of particular relevance to the present selection of Corneille's works – that the particular type of heroism analysed by Picard is not to be found in the early works. It is only in *The Place Royale* (1634) that we find the first traces of the conviction which was to pervade all his later plays – that the hero must retain his inner, moral independence, especially in love. The dominant note until then is 'a joyous lust for life, a certain cruelty, a pronounced taste for women in their simplest and most sensual aspects, a love for sword play and adventure'. There is no trace, for example, of his subsequent ideals in *The Theatrical Illusion*, which has the same freshness and fantasy as some of Shakespeare's comedies. In the same way, Corneille was uninhibited by the famous three unities which demanded that the central subject be closely knit, the scene unchanging, and the action confined to the space of twenty-four hours.

In *The Cid*, on the contrary, the new heroic ideal is the driving force in the minds and acts of the main characters, as Picard has so lucidly shown. But in that play there is such a powerful charge of youthful passion and excitement and such a balance between richness of episode and tautness of construction that the work is free from pompousness, unreal heroism or contrivance.

However, *The Cid*, though universally popular and the first masterpiece of the classical French stage, came under heavy fire from the playwright's rivals and was later submitted (in 1637) by Cardinal Richelieu to the newly founded French Academy (the literary establishment of the day) which was to act as an arbiter between the opposing factions. The Academy, though it tried hard to be fair, was in the main composed of 'the learned' who, while able to see the formal weaknesses of the work, were blind to its elemental greatness. Their findings praised Corneille warmly, but agreed with the critics that he had not observed the rules. Corneille was deeply hurt by the verdict, and his friend, Chapelain, found him two years later still obsessed by this issue and working out arguments to refute the Academy's strictures. Even in 1660, he was still trying in his critical writings to win a retrospective battle on this debate.

And hence, when he emerged from a three-year silence and produced *Horatius* and *Cinna* (in 1640), his craftsmanship, his choice of subject and his views had suffered a sea-change. True, he was always to maintain that he accepted the rules only to the extent that they suited him (but, as a modern writer has put it neatly, only once he had established what the rules were), but all his life, as far as he possibly could, he tried to stick to them, and often with the most disturbing results.

For his innate tendency was to cram his five acts with the most varied action, whereas the three unities are suited to the spare psychological tragedy where external action is reduced to the absolute minimum (as in Racine's works).

The same switch in emphasis is reflected in his subjects. Whereas both *The Cid* and *The Theatrical Illusion* are Spanish by inspiration and source, *Horatius* and *Cinna* (for the first time in Corneille's theatre) take place in ancient Rome. Of course, the change was not an absolute one, for Corneille by no means abandoned Spain as a quarry for dramatic themes. But that he veered in a different direction is clear.

And lastly, there is a difference in the political values underlying his work. In *The Cid*, even if we make the fullest allowances for the fact that the action takes place at the height of the Middle Ages in Spain when kings were by no means absolute, there is a distinct contrast between the image of the monarch in, say, *The Cid* and in *Cinna*. In the former play, the king is still very much *primus inter pares*. He is dependent on, and is defied by, his general (the Count) to a far greater degree than any other prince in Corneille's theatre, and certainly than Augustus. What is more, the spotlight in *The Cid* is focused on a mere knight – and a twenty-year-old stripling at that. On the other hand, the men who challenge the limitless power of Caesar (Cinna, Maximus and the rest) would be ignominiously swept into the discard of history were they not rescued by the equally limitless nobility of soul of the emperor. Here again, of course, it is not a question of a complete volte-face. Corneille retains his belief in the superiority of the concept of the king as a Christian knight, firm but merciful, as against that of the centralized monarchy and its Machiavellian ethos which was being sponsored by Richelieu. And the heroism which, from *The Cid* on, is a constant of his work is not only based on grandeur of soul, but is placed at the service of the romanesque ideal of honour.

'Romanesque', as the form of the word indicates, stands for the type of literature and ethos derived from the medieval romance, and hence impregnated with its spirit. The romanesque thus meant the far-fetched, the unusual, the adventurous, the ideal, often with a touch of the supernatural. The typical subjects were the exploits of knights errant – single combats and abductions. The guiding principle was that of honour and a romantic devotion to the beloved, and the ending was always a happy one. Much of the material for romanesque novels or plays was taken from Spain. (There was, it has been noted, a large Spanish colony in Corneille's native Rouen.) In this largely feudal world, nobility of soul and nobility of rank are broadly identical. If abstraction is made of this equation, however, the romanesque ethos of the early seventeenth century is disconcertingly similar to that of the cinema. There are also close analogies with the works of Shakespeare, and it is perhaps in this perspective that Corneille can best be appreciated by an Anglo-Saxon public. In fact, in the rare cases where the language barrier has been surmounted, the reaction of English and American readers is usually one of incredulous delight at finding a French classical dramatist in whose plays events actually happen and which do not consist simply of endless discussions.

Of Corneille the man, only the briefest account is called for. He was born of sound bourgeois stock in 1606 in the Norman town of Rouen, and, after studies with the Jesuits (who at the time had most of pre-University education in their hands), he entered the legal profession and practised till 1662 when he moved to Paris with his brother and fellow writer, Thomas. He was a model father to his seven children, though perhaps somewhat over-keen in soliciting pensions and favours, for example by obsequious dedications. He was also the first dramatist to treat his works as an important source of income, which shocked many of his contemporaries. He was awkward in speech and manner, but was always attracted, though within respectable limits, by women. He was justifiably proud of his works and fiercely aggressive in defending them against criticism. As Adam puts it, he had an unfortunate way of proving that he was right. He resented competition and used the 'Norman clan' (his brother and Donneau de Visé, who controlled much of the press at the time) to suppress his competitors such as the up-and-coming Racine, who referred to him waspishly as 'an ill-intentioned old playwright'. Corneille had small cause for such defensiveness, for he was the uncontested master of the dramatic scene. In 1663, a collected edition of his plays was published in two folio volumes – an honour usually reserved for the classics such as Virgil. He lived modestly, but there is no truth in the assertion that he died in poverty (1684, at the age of 78).

There is no obvious link between Corneille's life and theatre, unless we regard the latter as an escape from his relatively modest social position in an aristocratic world. He was a typical representative of his age in his attitudes, but he was highly untypical in his literary craftsmanship. To his inventive and inexhaustible dramatic genius must be added an infinite capacity for going over his works again and again, usually, but not always, with felicitous results, which, however, improved the clarity and impact of the lines rather than the music. If he lacks the harmony of Racine, he has a power and sonority which often, in the original, remind the listener of the finer flights of Elizabethan tragedy.

A fuller understanding of Corneille can be achieved only through a study of his works. In the Prefaces to the three plays that follow the reader will find an elaboration of most of the ideas set out in the present Introduction.

BIBLIOGRAPHY

The best introduction to Corneille in English is the section on the dramatist by Raymond Picard in his *Two Centuries of French Literature* (English translation, London, Weidenfeld and Nicolson, 1970), where the emphasis is on Corneille's wide variety and irrepressible originality. In French, readers should consult Georges Couton's works, and, to start with, his *Corneille*, revised edition, 1969. The chapters devoted to Corneille by Antoine Adam in his monumental *Histoire de la Littérature Française au XVIIe Siècle*, especially in Volume 1 (1948), are admirable. Other studies worth consulting are:

Paul Bénichou, *Morales du grand Siècle* (1948).

Louis Herland, *Corneille par lui-même* (1968). The title is misleading and the study somewhat garrulous, but stimulating and well illustrated.

Octave Nadal, *Le Sentiment de l'Amour dans l'Oeuvre de Pierre Corneille* (1948).

On a less academic level:

Robert Brasillach, *Corneille* (1938). An enthusiastic panegyric of the writer.

Jean Schlumberger, *Plaisir à Corneille* (1936). A delightful annotated anthology.

The school editions of the three plays in the present anthology, especially in the Classiques Larousse and (for *Le Cid* and *Cinna*) in the Petits Classiques Bordas, are models of what such presentations should be.

THE CID

PREFACE

The Cid, says Brasillach rightly, is 'unique in the French language'. It is the first masterpiece not only of the classical theatre but of Corneille himself. It has a youthful passionateness, exuberance and sureness of touch which the dramatist was never to recapture. It could well be said of the author as of the hero of the play:

> My equals burst but once upon the world,
> And their first blow displays their mastery.
> (lines 407–8)

The success of the work (first performed early in 1637) was immediate and overwhelming. It drew packed houses night after night, and, as Boileau put it some thirty years later,

> All Paris for Rodrigo [had] the eyes
> Of young Ximena.

The work was translated into English the same year as its appearance, and into all the other West European languages soon after, including Spanish (that version being long and mistakenly regarded as one of Corneille's sources). While enthusiasm outside France soon declined, the play is still a favourite of the Comédie Française, and indeed of the French stage in general.

Its success, especially at the time, was due not only to its sheer brilliance but also to the fact that it possessed a special appeal for the French public in the age of Louis XIII. For one thing, it was a tragi-comedy, which was the genre in fashion. The typical tragi-comedy had a happy ending, copious and varied action (including abductions, single combats and *coups de théâtre*), as well as harmonious outpourings of the despair of the heroes and heroines. Many of the subjects were borrowed from Spain, where the romanesque had always thrived, although this trend declined somewhat after 1635 when war broke out between France and that country.

Corneille was, then, following current fashion when he sought his inspiration in *Las Mocedades del Cid*, by Guillén de Castro, which had appeared in 1618. The young knight's martial adventures against the Moors and his picturesque romance with Ximena were perfect material for a tragi-comedy. If anything, there was too abundant a range of episodes to choose from. Corneille wisely pruned the lush undergrowth, cut out some of the cruder details, and focused attention on the young couple. However, his excisions still left ample traces of the wilder, southern and medieval mores. Corneille himself, writing admittedly at a time when French taste had further evolved in a classical direction, gently deplored two of the more highly-coloured incidents – Rodrigo's request to Ximena to kill him with his own sword and his refusal to fight to win in his duel with Don Sancho. The dramatist attributes both lapses to the influence of Spanish sources or atmosphere.

However, such minor flaws hardly weigh in the balance against Spain's major contribution to the play. Corneille, as Brasillach notes, turned away from the usual bookish models and made contact with a theatre which was still full of sap and alive with the passions of a violent race. He was lucky enough to chance on a work which provided him with a generous fund of heroic legends, complaints and ballads. He was never again to have the good fortune to draw on such an earthy, popular source. The ardour, vigour and intensity of Spain can be felt through the carapace of the alexandrines, and even in those passages not modelled on a Spanish original something of the fire and sparkle of the basic material comes through.

Nor is the French play too constrained by the three unities which were gradually being imposed by the 'learned' establishment – unities totally unsuited to the needs of the action-oriented tragi-comedy. The play can in fact best be conceived as a series of fourteen tableaux performed on a multiple, Shakespearian-type stage in which each panel represents one of the aspects of Seville. It is poles apart from the unchanging semi-abstract palace in which most of Racine's tragedies unfold. True, the action is confined to the regulation twenty-four hours, and each of the acts corresponds to a point of time (clearly indicated in the text) – from mid-day through the late afternoon, nightfall, ten o'clock the following morning, to the noonday heat.

What is more interesting than the degree of observance or otherwise of the unities, however, is the masterly alternation throughout the play of slow and rapid movements, except in the final act where all the various themes are gathered together and resolved in the concluding harmony. Brasillach is surely right when he talks of the 'perpetual musical and cinematographic vigour of the play'.

But the real artistic unity lies deeper than the technical surface. By a happy chance, Corneille's own evolution converged perfectly with the needs of the work. Hitherto, he had shown a predilection for 'violent passions and great and noble thoughts, but without any philosophy'. However, just before *The Cid*, he developed a conviction of the supreme importance of will-power and of the need to be emotionally independent. In *The Cid*, this desire for inner freedom is placed at the service of the current romanesque ideal (which imbued most works of the time, but in a rather purposeless way). By combining the two concepts, Corneille gave perfect form, for the first time, to the romanesque passion for honour. Both the young lovers are determined to be loyal not only to their family ties but also to their love for each other (of which an essential component is the admiration for their beloved's nobility and integrity). By sheer *élan* and will-power, they succeed, though often coming near despair. And thereby they offer a superb illustration of the exacting ethos by which the age lived.

However lucid they (and the other characters) may be, they are not inhuman automata who blindly follow the dictates of 'duty', but are buoyed up by their very belief in the rightness and beauty of their high ideals. They are in fact extremists to the extent that they are prepared, at whatever cost, to live up to their convictions. And the stuff of the Cornelian drama is the tension resulting from the inner conflicts unleashed by the demands placed on them by cruel circumstances. The result of the domination of the play by these moral imperatives is that the action flows from inner emotional sources and gives the various episodes a dramatic unity which was unknown in the tragi-comedy, where chance guided the erratic action. Thus, as Adam observes, *The Cid*, though a tragi-comedy, has all the virtues of a tragedy, and, in his calmer old age, Corneille was coolly to assert that it was in fact one.

Since the ideals described are typical of the late baroque, fairly uncentralized society, it is hardly surprising that *The Cid* portrays a typical feudal power-structure in which the king is merely *primus inter pares* and not the absolute monarch which Louis XIII was seeking to become with Richelieu's powerful assistance. Don Diego's conduct, in particular, is reminiscent of that of some of the great nobles of France (especially of the princes of the blood), and it is strange that more capital was not made by Corneille's critics of the Count's rebellion in the play. As it was, the main charges against him (ultimately endorsed in an attenuated form by the newly-formed French Academy) were that the style was imperfect, the construction irregular, and the characters' conduct in certain respects unbecoming. The verdict came as a shock to the proud and sensitive nature of the playwright. He was silent for three years, and, when he emerged from his tent, it was to compose a much more 'regular' type of play in which, though not nearly to the extent alleged by the Romantics, his extrovert and romantic impulses were forced into the strait-jacket of rules which were not suited to either his genius or the genres preferred by him. It must be admitted, however, that as a result of his new approach, he achieved a far greater degree of dramatic concentration and effect.

Ironically enough, the criticism most frequently levelled against the play was that the heroine was unchaste. 'What indecency,' the cry went up, 'for a well brought-up orphan girl to receive in her apartment at night time her father's murderer.' The criticism makes a modern reader smile, but it cannot be entirely laughed off as meaningless. For it should not be forgotten that the hero is only twenty and his beloved even less. And, though passing through the filter of fierce idealism, there emanates from the play an all-pervading sensuality. *The Cid*, said Brasillach, 'is a permanent scandal'. Or, perhaps more accurately, it is 'about adventurous youth in love with love and danger'.

If *The Cid* is read (or even better, viewed) in this spirit, there is every reason to expect that audiences everywhere will be as captivated by its excitement as by the almost equally youthful and idealistic Henry V of Shakespeare's drama.

THE CID SUMMARY

ACT ONE

XIMENA learns that her father, Don Gomez, Count of Gormas, and Rodrigo's father, Don Diego, both agree to the marriage between their children. The Infanta, the king's daughter, is secretly in love with Rodrigo, but, in view of the difference in their social status, she has stifled her passion and has deliberately steered Ximena towards him. Don Gomez, who expected to be appointed the Prince of Castile's tutor, is disappointed when he learns that Don Diego has received the coveted honour. The two meet. Don Gomez insults his successful rival. The aged Don Diego, in despair, urges his son to avenge him. Rodrigo is torn between his desire to kill the Count and his love for the Count's daughter.

ACT TWO

The Count, secure in the knowledge that the throne depends on his military prowess, refuses to apologize to Don Diego, despite the king's orders. Rodrigo challenges the Count. The news comes in that the young man has killed his opponent. Don Diego and Ximena appear simultaneously before the king to plead their cause (for and against Rodrigo).

ACT THREE

Don Rodrigo enters Ximena's house while she is absent and hides till she returns. Rodrigo emerges to offer her his head, but she refuses, and admits (discreetly) her love for him. Don Diego urges his son to lead a band of friends against the Moors who are planning to attack Seville.

ACT FOUR

Rodrigo defeats the Moors. He relates his victory to the king, but is ordered to leave when Ximena's entrance is announced. She is led to believe that Rodrigo has been killed in battle, and faints at the news. When she learns the truth, she again demands vengeance for her father. The king allows her to choose a champion to challenge Rodrigo, and she designates Don Sancho. The prize will be Ximena's hand.

ACT FIVE

Rodrigo says farewell to Ximena. He is resolved on meeting his death in the duel. Ximena urges him to live. The two men fight. Don Sancho comes back to report the outcome and, before he can even speak, is met with a torrent of abuse, since Ximena thinks that he has killed Rodrigo. The king disillusions her. Rodrigo has won, but spared his opponent and asked the vanquished knight to bear the news to the court. The king urges Ximena to pardon Rodrigo, leaving her a year's grace before she marries him in accordance with the terms of the duel.

DEDICATION TO MADAME DE COMBALET[1]

(1637)

Madame,

This living portrait which I offer you portrays a hero who is fairly easy to recognize by the laurels with which he covered himself. His life was one long succession of victories; his body, carried about by his army, won battles even after his death; and his name, after six hundred years, has again triumphed in France. He has had too favourable a reception to regret having crossed his country's frontiers and having learned to speak another language than his own. This outcome has surpassed my wildest expectations, and at first surprised me; but it ceased surprising me as soon as I saw the satisfaction you displayed when it was performed before you. Then I dared expect of him everything that took place, and I felt that, after the praises with which you had honoured him, this universal applause could not fail to be accorded to him. And, in fact, Madame, one cannot justly doubt the value of something that has been fortunate enough to please you. Your judgement on it guarantees its value; and, as you always liberally accord to real beauties the esteem they deserve, false beauties are never able to dazzle you. But your generosity is not confined to sterile praise for works which please you; it takes delight in extending itself usefully to those who write them, and does not disdain to employ in their favour the great influence which your rank and virtues have won you. I have experienced the results of your intervention which are too advantageous to me for me to pass them over in silence, and I owe you no less thanks for myself than for *The Cid*. This is a recognition which is to my credit, since it is impossible to announce that I am deeply obliged to you without at the same time announcing

1. Niece of Cardinal Richelieu, ruler of France at the time.

that you have had sufficient esteem for me to wish me to have these obligations to you. Thus, Madame, if I wish this success of my pen, this happy effort, to be fairly lasting, it is not for it to inform posterity of my name, but only to leave eternal proofs of what I owe you and to set before the eyes of those who will be born in centuries to come the protestation that I make to be all my life,

Madame,

Your very humble, very obedient and very devoted servant,

CORNEILLE

CAST

DON FERNANDO, *first King of Castile*

DOÑA URRACA, *Infanta of Castile*

DON DIEGO,[1] *Don Rodrigo's father*

DON GOMEZ, *Count of Gormas, Ximena's father*

DON RODRIGO, *Ximena's beloved*

DON SANCHO, *in love with Ximena*

DON ARIAS } *Castilian noblemen*
DON ALONSA }

XIMENA, *Don Gomez's daughter*

LEONORA, *the Infanta's governess*

ELVIRA, *Ximena's governess*

A PAGE *to the Infanta*

The scene is at Seville

1. Pronounced in two syllables as in Spanish.

THE CID

ACT ONE

Scene One

Ximena's apartment

XIMENA, ELVIRA

XIMENA

Is this account, Elvira, quite sincere?
Have you concealed nothing my father[1] said?

ELVIRA

I'm still enchanted by it. His esteem
Equals your passion for Rodrigo, and,
Unless I do not read his soul aright,
He will command you to return his[2] love.

XIMENA

Tell me, then, I implore you, once again,
What makes you think that he approves my choice.
Tell me afresh what hope I may conceive.
Such magic words cannot be heard too oft.
You cannot go too far in promising
Freedom to love each other openly.
What was your answer to the secret plea
Don Sancho and Rodrigo make to you?
Did you not show how much my heart inclines
To one of these two suitors for my hand?

ELVIRA

No. I depicted you indifferent,
Not swelling or destroying either's hopes

1. Don Gomez, Count of Gormas. 2. Don Rodrigo's.

And with an eye not cruel, but not kind,
As guided only by a father's choice.
He welcomed this respect. His words and looks
At once bore witness to his joy at it,
And, since I must again recount the tale,
These are his quick remarks on you and them.
'She does what's fitting. Both deserve her hand.
Both spring from valiant, loyal families.
They're young, but in their eyes already shines
The glorious mettle of their ancestors.
Above all, Don Rodrigo bears the mark
In every feature of high-heartedness.
His is a line so rich in warriors
That laurels decked their cradle and their youth.
His father's[1] valour, peerless in his day,
While strength was in him, all did marvel at.
His feats are graven on his wrinkled face
Which still reflects his might in former times.
The son may be what once his father was.
In short, he is a fitting match for her.'
The council whither he in haste was bound
Cut short his words hardly had they begun.
But even from what he said, I think his choice
Between your suitors hardly is in doubt.
The king must name a tutor for his son,
And such a signal honour is his[2] due.
The choice is not in doubt. His unexcelled
Valour can brook no fear of rivalry.
Just as his exploits are unparalleled,
He'll have no rival in his rightful hopes;
And, since Rodrigo has prevailed upon
His father to approach the Count at once,[3]
He[4] will select the fitting moment, and
All your desires will soon be satisfied.

1. Don Diego. 2. Don Gomez.
3. 'After the council' in the original. 4. Don Diego.

XIMENA

And yet it seems my anguished soul rejects
This happiness and bends beneath its weight;
The course of fate can in a moment change.
In this great joy I fear a great reverse.

ELVIRA

You'll see this fear most happily belied.

XIMENA

Let's wait the outcome, whatsoe'er it be.

Scene Two

The Infanta's apartment

THE INFANTA, LEONORA, THE PAGE

THE INFANTA

Page, bear this message to Ximena. Say
She waits too long to pay her call on me.
Tell her my friendship chides her tardiness.
(*The page goes back in*)

LEONORA

Each day the same desire oppresses you;
And in your talks with her I see each day
You ask her how her love is faring.

THE INFANTA

There
Are grounds for my concern. I almost forced
Her to return Rodrigo's passion If.
She loves Rodrigo, she is his through me;
Through me Rodrigo vanquished her disdain.
Thus, having forged the links that bind their hearts,
I must bestir myself to crown their bliss.

LEONORA

Lady, although success attends your plans,
You manifest excessive signs of care.
Is it the love that so enchants these two
That plunges you in sadness so profound?
And does your deep concern on their behalf
Make you unhappy in their happiness?
But I am indiscreet and go too far.

THE INFANTA

Hiding my sadness makes it twice as deep.
Listen. Oh! listen to my battles and
What fierce assaults my constancy sustains.
Love is a cruel tyrant, pitiless.
This youthful knight whom I bestowed on her,
I love him.

(*Leonora starts*)

THE INFANTA

Lay your hand upon my heart.
Feel how it falters at its victor's name,
And recognizes him.

LEONORA

Forgive me if,
Setting aside respect, I criticize.
Can a great princess so forget herself
As to admit a knight into her heart?
The king and all Castile, what will they say?
Are you still mindful of what stock you come?

THE INFANTA

So mindful am I that I'll shed my blood
Before I stoop to sullying my rank.
I might reply that, in the finest souls,
Merit alone should kindle passion's flame;

And, if my feelings were to seek excuse,
A thousand famous names would sanction them.
But I'll not do like them, if honour's stained.
The senses cannot take me by surprise;
I know that, as the daughter of a king,
None but a prince is worthy of my hand.
When I perceived my heart without defence,
Myself I gave that which I dared not take
And placed Ximena's heart where mine had been.
I fired their passion to put out my own.
Be not surprised then if my anguished soul
Impatiently awaits their nuptials. For
You see my inner peace depends thereon.
Love lives on hope, but perishes with it;
It is a fire that dies for lack of food;
Despite the harshness of my destiny,
If my Rodrigo and Ximena wed,
I shall be dead to hope but live at peace.
Meanwhile my torments are beyond belief;
Unwed, Rodrigo menaces my heart.
I strive to lose him but regret his loss;
That is the reason of my inner woe.
I grieve that love's assault obliges me
To pine, to languish for what I disdain;
I feel my very being rent in twain.
If my morale is high, my heart's on fire;
This marriage, feared and wished for, is my death;
I dare to hope from it but partial joy.
My glory and my love I treasure so
I'll die whether it's solemnized or not.

LEONORA

Lady, after these words all I can say
Is that I grieve to see your sufferings.
Before, I blamed you. Now I pity you.
But, since your virtue fights the magic power
Of this so sweet and poignant malady,

Repulses its attacks, rejects its spell,
It will restore calm to your faltering mind.
Put then your hope in that and healing time.
Expect all things from heaven. It is too fair
To leave your fortitude upon the rack.

THE INFANTA

My fondest hope is to be dead to hope.

THE PAGE

By your command, Ximena comes this way.

THE INFANTA (*to Leonora*)

Go. Entertain her in this gallery.

LEONORA

Will you remain deep in this sombre trance?

THE INFANTA

No. All I wish, despite my grieving heart,
Is somewhat to regain composure. Then
I'll follow you. (*Alone*) Just heavens, grant me your aid;
To my obsession set at last a bound.
Safeguard my honour and my peace of mind.
In others' happiness I seek my own.
Upon this marriage hang three destinies.
Make it come faster or my soul more strong.
Link by the marriage tie two loving hearts,
And end my torments, sundering my bonds.
But I delay. Let's to Ximena, and
By talking to her ease my tortured soul.

Scene Three

A public square in front of the royal palace

THE COUNT, DON DIEGO

THE COUNT

So you've prevailed. The favour of the king
Gives you a rank that's due to me alone –
The tutor of the Crown Prince of Castile!

DON DIEGO

This mark of honour to my family
Shows the king's just to all, and clearly proves
That he can well reward past services.

THE COUNT

Kings may be great, but they are men like us.
They can be wrong as other mortals are.
And this choice proves to all the courtiers
That kings reward not present services.

DON DIEGO

Let us forget a choice that angers you.
Favour may count as much as merit does.
But it's a duty to unbounded power
Not to examine what a king has willed.
Enhance the honour that's been done to me.
Let's link by sacred bonds my house and yours.
You've but one daughter; I have but one son.
Their marriage rites can make us more than friends.
Pray, Sir, accept him as your son-in-law.

THE COUNT

Let your fine son aspire to higher things.
The added splendour of your dignity
Should make his heart swell with a greater pride.
Discharge your office, educate your prince,

Instruct him how a kingdom must be ruled;
Make people quake beneath his laws, and fill
With love the good, with fear the wicked. Add
To all these virtues that of general.
Show him how to inure himself to pain,
In feats of Mars prove himself unexcelled,
Spend his whole days and nights on horseback, rest
In all his armour, force a city wall,
And all alone ensure the victory.
Teach him perfection by example and
Explain to him your lessons by your deeds.

DON DIEGO

If he would learn in spite of envy, he
Need only read the story of my life.
There, in the register of brilliant feats,
He'll see how nations have to be subdued,
How to attack a fort, array his troops,
And on great exploits build a great renown.

THE COUNT

Living examples are of much more power.
No prince can learn his duty in a book.
And what have you achieved in all these years
That I've not equalled in a single day?
If you were valiant, I am valiant still.
This arm is the king's trustiest support.
Granada, Aragon, quail at this sword;
My name serves as a rampart for Castile,
And, but for me, you'd bow to other laws,
And soon your enemies would be your kings.
Each day, each hour, adds to my glory, piles
Laurels on laurels, victory on victory.
The prince would at my side assay his sword
In battle under my protecting arm.
He'd learn to conquer as he watched me fight,
And, quickly to respond to his great soul,
He'd see . . .

DON DIEGO

I know how well you served the king.
I've seen you fight, commanding under me.
When age had chilled my sinews, fittingly
Your rare and well-tried valour took my place;
And, to dispense with pointless argument,
You are today as great as once I was.
You see that nonetheless a king has drawn
A certain difference between us two.

THE COUNT

Where I deserved to triumph, you prevailed.

DON DIEGO

Whoever won the post deserved it best.

THE COUNT

Who can discharge it best is worthiest.

DON DIEGO

To be refused the post is no good sign!

THE COUNT

You had it as a courtier by intrigue.

DON DIEGO

Only my glorious exploits spoke for me.

THE COUNT

Rather, the king does honour to your age.

DON DIEGO

The king's one standard is courageousness.

THE COUNT

The honour then was due to me alone.

DON DIEGO

Who was not given it deserves it not.

THE COUNT

Deserves it not! I?

DON DIEGO

You.

THE COUNT

Your impudence,
Reckless old man, will have its due reward.
(*He gives him a slap.*)

DON DIEGO (*drawing his sword*)

Go on and take my life after this slight –
The first at which my line has bowed in shame.

THE COUNT

And what, old weakling, could you hope to do?

DON DIEGO

O God! my failing strength abandons me!

THE COUNT

Your sword is mine, but it would swell your pride
If such a shameful prize burdened my hand.
Farewell! Despite of envy, let the prince
Be made to read the story of your life;
This fitting punishment of insolence
Will serve no little to adorn the tale.

Scene Four

DON DIEGO

O fury! O despair! O hostile age!
Have I then lived so long only for this?

Have I grown grey in warlike feats to see
My laurels faded in a single day?
My strong right arm the whole of Spain admires,
That arm which has so often saved the realm,
So many times buttressed a tottering throne,
Betrays me in my need, avails me nought.
O cruel memory of my past renown!
So many days in one day blotted out!
New honour fatal to my happiness!
O lofty heights from which my honour falls!
Must the Count's triumph dim my glory's rays?
Must I die unavenged or die in shame?
Count, be the prince's tutor. That high rank
Cannot be held by a dishonoured man;
Your jealous pride has, by this grave affront,
Made me, despite the king, unfit for it.
And you, the glorious sword of my exploits,
Are now an age-chilled body's ornament,
Once so much feared but used in this affront
Only for decoration, not defence,
Go, leave henceforth the lowest of the low.
Pass, to avenge me, into better hands.

Scene Five

DON DIEGO, DON RODRIGO

DON DIEGO

Are you a man, Rodrigo?

DON RODRIGO

Anyone
But you would learn at once I was!

DON DIEGO

Your wrath
And your response are music to my grief.
My blood speaks in this noble anger, and

Your blazing ardour gives me back my youth.
Come, O my son! my blood! wipe out my shame!
Avenge me . . .

(*Don Rodrigo starts*)

DON DIEGO

. . . of a cruel, harsh affront
Which deals our honours both a mortal blow.
A slap! It should have cost the man his life!
But age betrayed my noble-hearted urge!
And this my sword I can no longer wield,
I give to you to punish and revenge.
Assay your courage on base arrogance.
Such crimes can be effaced by blood alone.
Kill or be killed. But do not be deceived.
The foe assigned you is a fearful one.
I've seen him dripping blood, covered with mire,
Spreading affright throughout an army's ranks,
A hundred squadrons routed by his might.
And, to add yet one further detail, more
Than a brave captain, a great general,
He is . . .

DON RODRIGO

Finish.

DON DIEGO

Ximena's father.

DON RODRIGO

He's . . .

DON DIEGO

Do not reply. I know your love for her.
But life in infamy is worse than death.
A dear offender makes a great offence.
Now you have learned th' affront. Vengeance is yours.
I'll say no more. Avenge me and yourself.

Show that you are your father's worthy son.
Crushed by the ills in which fate plunges me,
I'll mourn. Go off, run, sweep to your revenge!

Scene Six

DON RODRIGO

Pierced to the heart
By such an unforeseen and mortal blow,
Hapless avenger of a just dispute
And wretched victim of an unjust fate,
I cannot stir, and my dumbfounded soul
Sinks under such a weight.
So near seeing my love returned,
O God! the agony.
It is my father who's offended, and
Ximena's father has offended him!

What battles fierce within!
Against my honour passion takes up arms.
If I avenge him, then I must lose *her*.
One fires me on. The other holds me back.
The shameful choice is to betray my love
Or live in infamy.
In either case, my grief is infinite.
O God! the agony.
I leave an insult unavenged
Or punish my belovèd's father.

Father, belovèd, honour, love,
Noble and harsh constraint, sweet tyranny;
My joy will die, or tarnished be my name.
One makes me wretched, *one* unfit to live.
Dear cruel hope of an aspiring soul –
A soul that's deep in love –
O worthy foe of my great happiness,
O sword, cause of my grief,

Are you to help me to achieve revenge,
Or to make sure Ximena's lost to me?

Better to haste to death.
My duty is to my belovéd, too.
Taking revenge, I earn her hate or wrath,
And, taking no revenge, I earn contempt.
One makes me faithless to my dearest hope,
One unworthy of her.
My ill increases if I seek a cure.
Everything swells my grief.
Come then my soul, and, since we have to die,
Let's die at least without offending her.

To die without revenge!
To seek a death fatal to my renown!
To suffer Spain to brand my memory
With a foul stigma that dishonours me!
To cherish still a love my frantic soul
Knows I am bound to lose!
I'll close my ears to these insidious thoughts,
Which merely fan despair.
Come, save at least my honour, strong right arm,
Since after all Ximena's loss is sure.

Yes, I was wrong.
My duty's to my father, not to her.
Whether I die from sword or broken heart,
I'll shed my blood as pure as at my birth.
I tax myself with being too remiss.
Let's hasten to revenge;
Deeply ashamed at having wavered so,
Let's hesitate no more,
Since it's my father who's offended and
Ximena's father has offended him.

ACT TWO

Scene One

A room in the palace

DON ARIAS, THE COUNT

THE COUNT

Between ourselves, yes, I was somewhat prompt,
Reacting to a word high-handedly.
But, being done, the deed's past remedy.

DON ARIAS

To the king's will your lion heart must yield.
He follows closely this affair; his might
In its full anger will descend on you.
In any case, Sir, you have no defence.
The victim's rank, the greatness of the offence,
Call for submission, for such deference,
No common reparations will suffice.

THE COUNT

My life is at the king's disposal.

DON ARIAS

Sir,
You were too headstrong after the affront.
The King still loves you; mitigate his wrath.
He's said: I wish it. Will you disobey?

THE COUNT

Sir, to preserve the honour of my name,
To disobey a little's no great crime.

However great the offence, my services
Should be enough to make him pardon it.

DON ARIAS

Whatever glorious deeds a subject does,
These never put the monarch in his debt.
You much deceive yourself, and you should know
Duty well done is service to the king.
This confidence will be your downfall, Sir.

THE COUNT

I shall believe you only when I fall.

DON ARIAS

You should redoubt the power of a king.

THE COUNT

One day cannot unseat a man like me.
Let all his[1] might assemble for my doom;
The State itself must perish if I die.

DON ARIAS

What! fear you not the sovereign sceptre's power?

THE COUNT

Which, but for me, would tumble from his hand.
His interest lies in keeping me alive;
If my heads falls, his throne will topple too.

DON ARIAS

Come, let your reason calm your spirits. Take
A sound decision.

THE COUNT

I have taken it.

DON ARIAS

What shall I say? I must report to him.

1. The king's.

THE COUNT

That I shall never tolerate disgrace.

DON ARIAS

Remember, kings wish to be absolute.

THE COUNT

The die is cast. Let's speak no more of it.

DON ARIAS

Farewell, then, since you cannot be convinced.
With all your laurels, fear the thunderbolt.

THE COUNT

I'll wait for it unbowed.

DON ARIAS

But not unscathed.

THE COUNT

Thereby we'll see Don Diego satisfied.

(*alone*)

Who fears not death is never moved by threats.
My heart's above the cruellest reverse.
They can reduce me to unhappiness,
But not persuade me to belie my name.

Scene Two

A public square in front of the royal palace

THE COUNT, DON RODRIGO

DON RODRIGO

Ho! Count, a word with you.

(*The Count turns round*)

DON RODRIGO

Settle a doubt.
You know Don Diego?

THE COUNT

Yes.

DON RODRIGO

And do you know
That this old man was bravery itself,
The valour and the glory of his time?

THE COUNT

Perhaps.

DON RODRIGO

This fire that flashes in my eyes,
Know you it is my father's?

THE COUNT

What of that?

DON RODRIGO

Four paces over there, I'll show you why.

THE COUNT

Presumptuous youth!

DON RODRIGO

Let not your choler rise.
I'm young, it's true, but, to aspiring hearts,
Valour's not measured by the count of years.

THE COUNT

You match yourself with *me*! What arrogance!
No one has ever seen you sword in hand.

DON RODRIGO

My equals burst but once upon the world,
And their first blow displays their mastery.

THE COUNT

Know you well who I am?

DON RODRIGO

Any but I
At your mere name would tremble with affright.
The laurels that lie thick upon your head
Seem to announce the sentence of my doom.
I rashly challenge a victorious arm,
But, since my heart is high, I've strength to spare.
T'avenge a father, naught's impossible.
Your arm's unconquered, not invincible.

THE COUNT

The mettle which your challenge to me shows
Was in your eyes to mine daily revealed.
Seeing in you the glory of Castile,
I gladly destined you my daughter's hand.
I know your love, and with delight I see
That all its ardour yields to duty still.
It has not weakened your high-heartedness;
Your self-dominion matches my esteem.
In making choice of you as son-in-law,
I did not err. You are a perfect knight.
But I am moved to spare you. I admire
Your spiritedness, pitying your youth.
Seek not to make a fatal trial, and
Dispense me from a short unequal fight.
This victory would yield me scant renown;
An easy triumph brings no glory. All
Would think that you were effortlessly slain,
And I would only have to mourn your death.

DON RODRIGO

Unworthy pity after such bold words!
Who takes my honour fears to take my life?

THE COUNT

Withdraw from here.

DON RODRIGO

Let's, waste no further words.

THE COUNT

You're tired of living?

DON RODRIGO

Do you fear to die?

THE COUNT

You do your duty. He who can outlive
His father's honour's an unworthy son.

Scene Three

The Infanta's apartment

THE INFANTA, XIMENA, LEONORA

THE INFANTA

Allay, Ximena, your despair, and rouse
Your resolution in adversity.
Calm will return after this sudden squall.
Your happiness is clouded over, but
You have lost nothing by a short delay.

XIMENA

My worry-laden heart dares hope for nought.
A storm so sudden that disturbs my calm
Is fraught with certainty of shipwreck. Now

There is no doubt. I perish safe in port.
I loved, was loved; our fathers were agreed,
And I was telling you th'enchanting news
The very moment this dispute arose,
Whose fatal course, no sooner was it told,
Ruined the outcome of my dearest hopes.
Accursed ambition, hateful lunacy,
Which tyrannizes over noblest hearts!
O honour! ruthless to my heart's desires.
How many sighs and tears you'll wring from me!

THE INFANTA

In their dispute you have no ground for fear.
A moment fired it and will put it out.
It has caused too much stir not to be quelled.
The king already seeks to reconcile
The two. And I who feel for your despair
Will do my best to find a remedy.

XIMENA

But reconciliation will not help.
Affronts to honour cannot be redressed.
In vain the king tries strength or cautiousness;
The ill is cured, but only seemingly.
The hatreds which are kept within us feed
Fires which, when hidden, all the fiercer burn.

THE INFANTA

The sacred tie that joins Rodrigo and
Ximena will dispel their fathers' hate,
And soon we'll see your love all the more strong
In happy marriage stifle this discord.

XIMENA

I wish it thus, more than I hope for it.
I know my father, and Don Diego's proud.
I feel the tears that I can not restrain.
The past is torture and the future black.

THE INFANTA

What do you fear? a weak old man's revenge?

XIMENA

Rodrigo is so valiant.

THE INFANTA

But too young.

XIMENA

A young man's valour shows in his first blow.

THE INFANTA

You must, however, not be too afraid.
He loves you so, that he will heed your wish,
And one word from your lips will check his wrath.

XIMENA

If he obeys me not, what grief is mine?
If he obeys, what will they say of him?
A man like him, to suffer such a slight!
Whether or not he yields to love for me,
I can be only shamefaced or distraught
At his respectful Yes or rightful No.

THE INFANTA

Ximena's noble and, although in love,
She cannot tolerate a craven thought.
But if, until the two are reconciled,
I make her perfect suitor prisoner
And step between his courage and his foe,
Will you, his sweetheart, not take umbrage?

XIMENA

Ah!
My worries in that case would have an end.

Scene Four

THE INFANTA, XIMENA, LEONORA, PAGE

THE INFANTA

Page, go and find Rodrigo. Bring him here.

THE PAGE

The Count and he . . .

XIMENA

O God, I tremble!

THE INFANTA

Speak.

THE PAGE

Together from this palace they went out.

XIMENA

Alone?

THE PAGE

Alone, and softly quarrelling.

XIMENA

It's clear they're fighting. Speak no more of it.
Forgive me if I leave so suddenly.

Scene Five

THE INFANTA, LEONORA

THE INFANTA

Alas! what deep disquiet stirs my heart.
I weep for her but worship her beloved.

My peace of mind is lost, my love revives.
Rodrigo from Ximena parted gives
New life to hope and yet to agony.
This rift between them which I sorrow for
Yet spreads a secret pleasure in my mind.

LEONORA

Your lofty virtue reigning in your soul
Hastes to surrender to this craven love?

THE INFANTA

Call it not craven now that in my heart
Proud and triumphant it dictates to me.
Show it respect since it's so dear to me.
Virtue resists: and yet I hope for it;
And, pandering to this insensate hope,
I seek a sweetheart that Ximena's lost.

LEONORA

Can you discard this glorious constancy;
Can reason in your soul thus abdicate?

THE INFANTA

How ineffectively does reason curb
The heart a magic potion acts upon!
And, when the patient loves the malady,
How hard he finds it to permit the cure!

LEONORA

Your hope leads you astray. You love your ill.
But he's unworthy of you.

THE INFANTA

That I know,
But, if my glory yields, it is because
Passion deceives a heart possessed by it.
If once Rodrigo conquers in the fight,

If to his valour this great warrior falls,
I can esteem him, love him without shame.
He can do all if he defeats the Count.
In thought I see that, at his least exploits,
Whole realms will fall and pass beneath his sway,
And my fond love already pictures him
Seated upon Granada's mighty throne,
The Moors, subdued, trembling, adoring him,
Aragon hailing this new conqueror,
Portugal yielding, and his noble feats
Beyond the seas swelling his destinies,
His laurels red with blood of Africans.
All that is told of warriors most renowned,
That I expect after this victory,
And glory in the love I feel for him.

LEONORA

How far, my lady, you project his power,
Based on a combat which may not take place!

THE INFANTA

Rodrigo was affronted by the Count!
The two of them went out. What need you more?

LEONORA

Well, they'll do battle, since you'll have it so,
But will Rodrigo really rise so high?

THE INFANTA

What would you? I am mad. My mind's distraught.
You see what ills this passion holds in store.
Come to my chamber. Soothe my aching heart,
And do not leave me in my present plight.

Scene Six

The king's apartment

DON FERNANDO, DON ARIAS, DON SANCHO

DON FERNANDO

The Count is so wrong-headed, arrogant?
He still dares think his crime can be forgiven?

DON ARIAS

I have on your behalf long talked with him.
I did my utmost, but to no effect.

DON FERNANDO

Heavens! this overweening subject, then,
So lacks respect or eagerness to please
He slights Don Diego and he scorns his king.
Here in my court he even dictates to me.
He may be brave and a great general,
But I will take his haughty humour down.
Were he great Mars himself, the god of war,
He'll see what it can mean, not to obey.
Although such insolence deserved its due,
I wished at first not to use violence.
But, since he takes advantage of it, go,
Detain him, whether he resists or not.

DON SANCHO

Perhaps a few days' grace would bow his will.
We caught him all on fire from his dispute.
Sire, in the heat of his first fighting mood,
So mettlesome a spirit cannot yield.
He sees he's wrong, but such a lofty soul
Will not at once admit to his offence.

DON FERNANDO

Silence, Don Sancho, and be warned by me
That it is criminal to take his side.

DON SANCHO

I shall obey. And yet, allow me, Sire,
A word in his defence.

DON FERNANDO

What's there to say?

DON SANCHO

That a great soul accustomed to great deeds
Can never stoop to tamely giving in.
It cannot without shame conceive of it,
And it's this word alone the Count resists.
He finds what duty orders somewhat harsh,
And would obey were he less mettlesome.
Command his arm, grown mighty in the wars,
To make amends at swordpoint. You will find
He will obey you, Sire, and, come what may,
I'll answer for him till he's heard of it.

DON FERNANDO

You lack respect, but I forgive your years,
And I excuse ardour in youthful hearts.
A king whose wisdom aims at better things
Is far more sparing of his subject's blood.
I watch over my people, keep them safe,
As does the head the members serving it.
So what is right for you is wrong for me.
You speak as soldier. I must act as king.
Whatever one may say and he dare think,
There's no dishonour in obeying me.
Besides, the affront is mine. He has disgraced
The man I made the tutor of my son.
To slight my choice is to attack myself
And seek to weaken my authority.
Let's talk no more of this. Ten vessels tall
Of our old enemies have hoist their flag,
Daring to sail up to the river's mouth.

DON ARIAS

The Moors have learned perforce to know you, Sire.
Vanquished so often, they have lost the drive
To challenge such a glorious conqueror.

DON FERNANDO

They'll never see without some jealousy
My sceptre govern Andalusia,
And this fair country, long possessed by them,
They'll always cast an envious eye on it.
This is the only reason why I chose
Seville as capital ten years ago –
To keep a closer watch on them and foil
Whatever moves they make, more rapidly.

DON ARIAS

They know, at their best generals' expense,
How much your presence leads to conquest, Sire.
You've naught to fear.

DON FERNANDO

And nothing to neglect.
Danger is bred of over-confidence,
And well you know that, with an easy oar,
A flowing sea-tide brings them up to here.
And yet it would be wrong of me to spread
Panic, since the report is not confirmed.
The fear this needless warning would arouse
As night is falling would confuse the town.
Double the guard on harbour and on walls.
This will be all tonight.

Scene Seven

DON FERNANDO, DON SANCHO, DON ALONSO

DON ALONSO

The Count is dead.
Don Diego by his son has been avenged.

DON FERNANDO

Vengeance was bound to follow the affront.
I tried, right from the start, to ward it off.

DON ALONSO

Ximena at your feet presents her suit.
She comes demanding justice, bathed in tears.

DON FERNANDO

Although my heart feels for her sufferings,
What the Count did appears to have deserved
This punishment of his temerity.
However fair though this revenge may be,
I cannot gladly lose a man like him.
He long has rendered service to the State;
A thousand times he's shed his blood for me;
Whatever I must feel about his pride,
His death distresses me and saps my power.

Scene Eight

DON FERNANDO, DON DIEGO, XIMENA,
DON SANCHO, DON ARIAS, DON ALONSO

XIMENA

Justice, Sire, justice!

DON DIEGO

Listen to us, Sire.

XIMENA

I'm prostrate at your feet.

DON DIEGO

I clasp your knees.

XIMENA

I demand justice.

DON DIEGO

Sire, hear my defence.

XIMENA

Punish a hothead and his insolence.
He has destroyed the pillar of your throne.
He's killed my father.

DON DIEGO

He's avenged his own.

XIMENA

A king owes justice to his subject's blood.

DON DIEGO

For righteous vengeance there's no punishment.

DON FERNANDO

Rise both of you and take your time to speak.
Ximena, I commiserate with you.
My sorrow is as grievous as your own.
(*To Don Diego*)
You will speak later. Do not interrupt.

XIMENA

My father's dead. My eyes have seen his blood
Gush from his great, his noble-hearted side,
This blood so oft the safeguard of your walls,
This blood, so oft battle-victorious,
This blood, though spilt, that reeks with anger still
At being shed for others than yourself,
That even war's hazards did not dare to draw,
Rodrigo in your court covers the earth
With it. I hurried hither, pale, distraught.
I found him lifeless, Sire; forgive my grief.
My voice fails as I tell this fearful tale.
My tears, more eloquent, can say the rest.

DON FERNANDO

Courage, my daughter. Know that, from today,
Your king will be your father in his stead.

XIMENA

Sire, you do too much honour to my woe.
I found him lifeless, as I said. His flank
Was open wide. The more to stir me on,
His blood had writ my duty in the dust.
Rather, his valour, now reduced so low,
Spoke to me through his wound, called for revenge.
And, to appeal to the most just of kings,
Borrowed by these unspeaking lips my voice.
Suffer not, under your authority,
That licence reign before your very eyes,
That even the bravest with impunity
Be offered up to overweening blows,
That a young hothead triumph over them,
Bathe in their blood and mock their memory.
A warrior such as he, ravished from you,
Will, unavenged, affect men's loyalty.
In short, my father's dead. Vengeance I cry
More in your interest than for my relief.

You suffer by the death of such a man.
Avenge it by another's, blood for blood.
Sacrifice not to *me*, but to your crown,
And to your greatness, to your person, Sire;
Sacrifice to the welfare of the State
All that so great an outrage swells with pride.

DON FERNANDO

Reply, Don Diego.

DON DIEGO

How I envy those
Who, losing strength, can also lose their life,
And how old age prepares a wretched fate
For noble men on ending their career.
I whose long labours have acquired me fame,
I who of old was wooed by victory,
Today, because I have outlived my time,
Have been affronted and have known defeat.
What never combat, ambush, siege achieved,
And never Aragon, Granada and
My foes unnumbered, all who envied me,
The Count did here, almost before your eyes,
Jealous of whom you chose, proud of the lead
My age's frailty gave him over me.
Thus would my hair, whitened in battle, Sire,
This blood so often lavished in your cause,
This arm – the terror of your enemies –
Have reached the tomb, laden with infamy,
Had I not bred a son worthy of me,
Worthy of Spain and worthy of my king.
He lent his hand to me, he killed the Count.
He gave me honour back, wiped out my shame.
If showing bravery and anger, if
Avenging insults merits punishment,
On me alone must fall the gathering storm.
When th'arm offends, one punishes the head.
Whether one calls our strife a crime or not,

I am the head; he, Sire, is but the arm.
If she declares he caused her father's death,
He'd not have done it were I able to.
Sacrifice then this head that age will reap,
And take, to fight for you, Rodrigo's arm.
Appease Ximena at my blood's expense.
I'll not resist. I'll gladly be condemned,
And, far from murmuring at a harsh decree,
Dying with honour, die without regret.

DON FERNANDO

This issue's weighty, and I deem it fit
To be debated by my counsellors.
Don Sancho, take Ximena to her home.
Don Diego is a prisoner in my court.
Bring me Rodrigo. Justice will be done.

XIMENA

It's right, great king, for murderers to die.

DON FERNANDO

Go, rest, my daughter, and appease your grief.

XIMENA

To bid me rest is to augment my woes.

ACT THREE

Scene One

Ximena's apartment

DON RODRIGO, ELVIRA

ELVIRA

Wretched Rodrigo, what has brought you here?

DON RODRIGO

I follow my ill-omened destiny.

ELVIRA

Whence this presumption, this fresh show of pride,
Here in a house you fill with mourning, Sir?
Even here you brave the Count of Gormas' shade.
You killed him.

DON RODRIGO

He disgraced me while he lived.
Honour demanded what my hand has done.

ELVIRA

You seek asylum in a dead man's house!
Never did murderer find a refuge there.

DON RODRIGO

I come but to surrender to my judge.
Cease to behold me with astounded gaze.
Here I seek death after inflicting it.
My judge is my Ximena, is my love.
I merit death as I deserve her hate,

And I'll receive it as the greatest boon
When she pronounces it and executes.

ELVIRA

Flee rather from her hand, flee from her wrath;
Escape her first wild fit of violence;
Do not expose yourself to the assault
Of the fierce outbursts of her anger. Go.

DON RODRIGO

No, no. My sweetheart whom I have displeased
Cannot demand too urgently my end,
And I'll avoid a hundred deaths if I
Can swell her anger and the sooner die.

ELVIRA

Ximena's at the palace bathed in tears,
And will come back fully accompanied.
Rodrigo, flee. Deliver me from care.
What will they say if they should see you here?
Would you have slander say, O crowning woe!
'Here she received her father's murderer'?
She will come back. She's coming. Here she is.
At least, Rodrigo, for her honour, hide.

Scene Two

DON SANCHO, XIMENA, ELVIRA

DON SANCHO

Yes, you need victims, Lady, you need blood.
Your anger's just, your tears legitimate,
And I'll not seek by dint of arguing
Either to calm you or console you. But,
If I can be of service to you, pray
Employ my sword to strike the offender down;

Employ my passion to avenge this death.
Fighting for you, my strength will know no bounds.

XIMENA

Unhappy that I am!

DON SANCHO

Accept my aid.

XIMENA

I would offend the King who's promised me
Justice.

DON SANCHO

Justice is halting, as you know,
For often crime escapes through its delays.
Its slow and doubtful course is strewn with tears.
Allow a knight to fight for your revenge –
A safer, quicker road to punishment.

XIMENA

That should serve only as a last resort.
But, if we must, and you still pity me,
You will be free then to avenge my wrongs.

DON SANCHO

To that sole happiness I now aspire.
Since I can hope for that, I am content.

Scene Three

XIMENA, ELVIRA

XIMENA

At last I'm free and can without constraint
Give vent to all my poignant sufferings.
I can indulge in melancholy sighs,

Opening my soul and all my woes to you.
My father's dead, Elvira. The first sword
Rodrigo wielded cut his thread of life.
Weep, weep, my eyes, dissolve. Half of my life
Has sent the other half down to the tomb,
And forces me thereafter to avenge
The one that's gone on the surviving one.

ELVIRA

Compose yourself.

XIMENA

Ah! how unfittingly
You urge, in such misfortune, fortitude.
How can my sorrow ever be appeased
If hating not the hand that causes it?
What can I hope for but eternal pain
If, fighting crime, I love the criminal?

ELVIRA

You love him still, he who unfathered you?

XIMENA

I love, Elvira, nay, I worship him.
My passion and my anger are at odds.
I find my sweetheart in my enemy,
And still I feel in spite of all my wrath
Rodrigo fights my father in my heart,
Attacks, strikes home, gives ground, defends himself,
Now strong, now weak and now triumphantly;
But, in this combat between love and wrath,
He rends my heart, but does not bend my will.
Whatever power my love has over me,
I will not shrink from doing what is right.
I go unwavering where my duty calls.
Rodrigo's dear to me. Would he were not!
Despite my passion which takes sides with him.
I am the daughter of the man he killed.

ELVIRA

You seek his downfall?

XIMENA

Ah, unnerving thought!
Cruel pursuit to which I am compelled!
I fear the punishment I ask for him.
My death will follow his which I demand.

ELVIRA

Abandon, lady, such a tragic plan.
Impose not on yourself so harsh a law.

XIMENA

My father dying, almost in my arms,
Cries out for vengeance and will not be heard?
My heart, surrendering to other lures,
Will owe him only ineffectual tears?
And I shall suffer a suborning love
To stifle thus my honour cravenly?

ELVIRA

Lady, believe me, you're excusable
For having failed to hound the man you love.
Against a sweetheart you have done enough.
You've seen the king. Do not yet press for deeds.
Do not persist in this strange mood of yours.

XIMENA

My name's at stake. I must avenge myself;
However much affection may beguile,
There can be no excuse for noble minds.

ELVIRA

But, loving him, you cannot disapprove.

XIMENA

True.

ELVIRA

In the end, what do you plan to do?

XIMENA

Preserve my glory, finish my despair,
Procure his doom and die when he is dead.

Scene Four

DON RODRIGO, XIMENA, ELVIRA

DON RODRIGO

Well, then, to save you from continuing,
Come, seize the honour of despatching me.

XIMENA

Elvira, what is this? what do I see?
Rodrigo in my house? Rodrigo here?

DON RODRIGO

Spare me not, for I'll not resist. Enjoy without regret
The sweetness of your vengeance and my death.

XIMENA

Alas!

DON RODRIGO

Hear me.

XIMENA

I die.

DON RODRIGO

A moment.

XIMENA

Go.
Leave me to die.

DON RODRIGO

Four words. Only four words.
Afterwards, answer only with this sword.

XIMENA

What! even though dripping with my father's blood?

DON RODRIGO

Ximena . . .

XIMENA

Take away that hated sword
Proclaiming your survival and your crime.

DON RODRIGO

Behold it rather to inflame your hate,
To swell your wrath and speed my punishment.

XIMENA

It's tainted with my blood.

DON RODRIGO

Plunge it in mine.
And thus efface the stain of your own blood.

XIMENA

What cruelty that kills in one same day
Father by sword, and daughter by its sight!
Remove this weapon that I cannot bear.
You wish a hearing, yet would make me die.

DON RODRIGO

I do your bidding, but I still desire
To have my sad life ended at your hands.
For in a word do not expect of me

Craven repentance for a rightful deed.
Your father's action, irreparable,
Disgraced my father, covering me with shame.
A man of honour's outraged by a slap;
I shared in the affront, sought out the Count,
And I avenged my father and my name.
I'd do it, were it to be done, again.
Not that against my father and myself
My love did not fight hard on your behalf.
Judge of its power when the offence was such
I wavered long whether to take revenge.
Forced to displease you or accept a slight,
I thought that in my turn I was too prompt.
I taxed myself with wild impetuousness;
And you would certainly have tipped the scales
Had I not set against your charms the thought
That I, dishonoured, did not merit you,
That, though I shared in your affection, yet
Who loved me brave would hate me infamous;
That to obey, and listen to your love,
Would make me quite unworthy of your choice.
I say again, and, though it tortures me,
I will repeat it till the day I die:
I have offended you; I *had* to strike
To cancel my disgrace and merit you;
Father and honour have received their due.
I can give satisfaction now to *you*.
You see me here to offer you my blood.
I did my duty, and I do it now.
A father dead arms you against my crime.
I shall not rob you of your victim. Strike.
Sacrifice firmly to the blood he lost
The one who glories in his victim's death.

XIMENA

Rodrigo. Ah! it's true. Although your foe,
I cannot blame your 'No' to infamy,
And, whatsoever form my grief may take,

I'll not accuse you; I bewail my woes.
I know what honour, after such a slight,
Demanded of a gallant-hearted knight.
You only did what duty bade you do,
But yet, by doing it, you taught me mine.
Your fateful valour guides my path. It has
Avenged your father, kept your name unstained.
I must do likewise and I must maintain
My glory and avenge my father dead.
Alas! my love for you makes me despair.
If by some other hand I was bereaved,
I would have, in the joy of seeing you,
Found the one balm that was acceptable.
I would have found relief for my despair,
When such belovéd hands had dried my tears.
But I must lose you after losing him.
My honour wills this effort by my love.
This hideous duty harries me to death
And forces me to have your life destroyed.
For from my passion, Sir, do not expect.
A craven shrinking from your punishment.
Whate'er our love may plead on your behalf,
My noble-heartedness must equal yours.
By wronging me, you're worthy of my hand.
I must be worthy of you by your death.

DON RODRIGO

Delay no more to do what honour bids.
Honour demands my life. I give it you.
Come, sacrifice me to this noble cause.
I'll welcome both the blow and the decree.
To wait on halting justice for revenge
Is to postpone your glory and my end.
I would die happy from so fine a blow.

XIMENA

I wish to prosecute, not execute.
Is it for *me* to lop your proffered head?

I must attack, you must defend yourself.
I must obtain it from another's hand.
I must pursue you but not punish you.

DON RODRIGO

Whatever thoughts our love inspires in you,
Your noble-heartedness must equal mine.
To borrow others' arms for your revenge,
Believe me, means you do not equal it.
My hand alone revenged my father's blood.
Your hand alone must take revenge for yours.

XIMENA

Cruel one! why insist on helping me,
You struck unaided and would give me aid.
I'll follow your example and refuse
To let my glory's fame be shared with you.
My father and my honour must not owe
Aught to affection or to your despair.

DON RODRIGO

O unrelenting honour! can I not
Ever obtain this favour from your hand.
Come. For a father's sake or for our love,
Punish me out of vengeance, or at least
For pity's sake. My anguish will be less,
Dead by your hand than living with your hate.

XIMENA

I hate you not.

DON RODRIGO

You ought to.

XIMENA

I can not.

DON RODRIGO

Do you not fear censure and lying tongues?
Knowing my crime and that our love endures,
What will not envy and imposture spread?
Force them to silence without more ado.
By putting me to death, save your repute.

XIMENA

It shines more bright by leaving you alive.
I want the voice of blackest jealousy
To praise my glory and deplore my woes,
Knowing I love you and desire your death.
Be off, and show not to my frantic grief
What I must forfeit though I love it still.
In darkest night hide your departure well.
If you are seen, my honour is at stake.
The only chance that calumny will have
Is to proclaim that I received you here.
Give it no opening to besmirch my name.

DON RODRIGO

I'd sooner die.

XIMENA

Go.

DON RODRIGO

What have you resolved?

XIMENA

Despite this passion which obscures my wrath,
I'll do my utmost to secure revenge.
But, notwithstanding duty's stern command,
My only wish is to be powerless.

DON RODRIGO

O miracle of love!

XIMENA

O crowning woe!

DON RODRIGO

How many ills our fathers dead will cause!

XIMENA

Who would have thought so?

DON RODRIGO

Who'd have said so?

XIMENA

Ah!

Our happiness so near was lost so soon.

DON RODRIGO

So near to land, against all likelihood,
A storm so sudden has dispelled our hopes.

XIMENA

Ah mortal grief!

DON RODRIGO

Ah pointless, vain regrets!

XIMENA

Once more, be off. I'll list no more to you.

DON RODRIGO

Farewell. I shall drag out a dying life
Until I am bereft of it through you.

XIMENA

If I attain that end, I pledge my word
Not to draw breath a moment after you.
Farewell. Go. And take care not to be seen.

ELVIRA

Lady, whatever ills heaven plagues you with ...

XIMENA

Importune me no more, but let me grieve.
I shall seek silence and the night to weep.

Scene Five

A public square in front of the royal palace

DON DIEGO

We never taste of bliss that's unalloyed.
Sadness attends our happiest success.
Always on these occasions some dark cares
Ruffle the surface of our limpid joy.
Midst happiness I feel care's icy hand.
I'm overjoyed but tremble yet with fear.
The foe who slighted me has met his death,
But I see not my son's avenging hand.
In vain I strive, and unavailingly
Exhausted as I am I search the town.
The last faint vigour of my ancient years,
Seeking my son, is fruitlessly consumed.
At every moment in so dark a night,
I would embrace him – and embrace a shade.
My love, cheated by this deceiving veil,
Conjures up visions which increase my dread.
Discovering no traces of his flight,
I fear the dead man's friends and retinue.
Their numbers terrify and fluster me.
Rodrigo lives no more or lives in gaol.
Merciful heavens! do I see aright?
Or do I see at last my only hope?
It's he. I doubt no more. My prayer's fulfilled,
My fear's dispelled, my suffering's at an end.

Scene Six

DON DIEGO, DON RODRIGO

DON DIEGO

Rodrigo! you're at last vouchsafed to me.

DON RODRIGO

Alas!

DON DIEGO

Come, mingle not my joy with sighs.
Let me recover breath to sing your praise.
My valour cannot disavow your deed.
You've equalled it. There lives in you again
The daring of the heroes of my line.
If you descend from them, you're bred by me.
The first blow of your sword's worth all of mine,
And, fired by glorious gallantry, your youth
At this first effort equals my renown.
Pillar of my old age, my crowning joy,
Touch these white hairs whose honour you've restored.
Come, kiss this cheek and recognize the spot
Of the affront your courage has effaced.

DON RODRIGO

The honour was your due. I could no less,
Since I'm your flesh and blood, and bred by you.
I am delighted my beginner's blow
Has pleased the man whose lifeblood runs in me.
But in your joy do not begrudge me this,
That in my turn I dare to speak my mind.
Suffer me to indulge in my despair.
Enough have you beguiled it, nay, too long.
I'll not repent of having served you well,
But give me what my blow bereft me of.
My arm fought in your cause against my love,

And by this blow has robbed me of my soul.
Say nothing more; for *you* I have lost all.
I have repaid in full my debt to you.

DON DIEGO

Carry your victory still further. Think
I gave you life; you gave me back my name.
And, since I cherish glory more than life,
My debt to you is all the heavier.
But from your heart remove such weaknesses.
There's but one honour; mistresses[1] abound!
Love's but a pleasure; duty's a command.

DON RODRIGO

What say you, father?

DON DIEGO

What you ought to know.

DON RODRIGO

My honour was avenged upon myself!
And you dare urge me to inconstancy!
Like[2] infamy weighs equally upon
The craven warrior and the faithless heart.
Do not this wrong to my fidelity.
Let me be chivalrous but not for sworn.
My ties are strong and are not broken thus;
My troth still holds, even if I hope no more.
And, since I cannot win or leave my love,
The death I seek will be the sweetest pain.

DON DIEGO

The time has not yet come to seek your death;
Your monarch and your country need your arm.
The fleet we feared is in the river, plans
To fall upon the town and pillage it.

1. In the seventeenth-century sense of the woman who is loved.
2. In the sense of equal.

Within an hour, the floodtide and the night
Up to our walls will bring them soundlessly.
The court's in disarray, the people fear.
All that one hears are cries and sees are tears.
In this grave crisis, fortune has so willed
That in my house five hundred friends have met
Who, learning my affront, with equal zeal
Streamed hither, eager to support my cause.
You had forestalled them, but your valiant hands
Would find in Moorish blood a better prize.
As their commander, go where honour calls.
You are the leader these brave men demand.
Go. Meet the onslaught of your foes of old.
There, if you wish, you'll find a glorious death,
Seize the occasion which is offered you.
Let the king owe salvation to your death,
Or come back rather, laurels on your brow.
Do not confine your glory to revenge.
Carry it further by your valiance. Force
Ximena and the king to pardon you.
If you still love her, learn that victory
Is the one way of winning back her heart.
But time's too precious to be lost in words.
I but delay you when I'd give you wings.
Come, follow me, to fight and show your king
What in the Count he's lost, he's gained in you.

ACT FOUR

Scene One

Ximena's apartment

XIMENA, ELVIRA

XIMENA

It's not a false report? It's really true?

ELVIRA

It's not to be believed how he's admired.
With one consent they praise him to the skies,
And laud the hero's glorious feats of arms.
The Moors were routed by him; their attack
Was sudden, but more sudden was their flight.
Three hours of battle left our warriors
With total victory and two captive kings.
Their leader swept aside all obstacles.

XIMENA

Rodrigo's hand worked all these miracles?

ELVIRA

These two kings are the prize of his great deeds.
His hand defeated them and captured them.

XIMENA

Who told you all this extraordinary news?

ELVIRA

The common folk who sing his praises and
Call him the cause and object of their joy,
Their guardian angel and their rescuer.

XIMENA

How does the king regard such prowesses?

ELVIRA

Rodrigo dares not yet appear in court;
But old Don Diego, in the victor's name,
Transported, offers him these kings in chains
And asks the favour of our noble prince
To deign to see the knight who saved his realm.

XIMENA

He is not wounded?

ELVIRA

I have no such news.
Your colour changes. Calm yourself. Revive.

XIMENA

Let me revive rather my flagging wrath.
Must I forget myself and feel concern?
He's praised, he's vaunted, and my heart applauds!
My honour mute, my anger powerless!
Silence, then, love! Bring honour to the fore.
If he's enslaved two kings, he's killed the Count,
And these sad garments which proclaim my woe
Are the first outcome of his gallantry.
Elsewhere this lionheart may be extolled;
Everything here speaks to me of his crime.
You who restore strength to my failing wrath,
Veil, mourning and funereal ornaments,
This pomp prescribed by his first victory,
Sustain my glory now against my love.
And, when my passion gains the upper hand,
Remind me of my duty's sad command;
Attack undaunted a triumphant arm.

ELVIRA

Restrain your outbursts. The Infanta's here.

Scene Two

THE INFANTA, XIMENA, LEONORA, ELVIRA

THE INFANTA

I come not hither to condole with you,
But to commingle with your tears my sighs.

XIMENA

Share rather in the universal joy
And taste the happiness that heaven sends.
No one but I has any right to grieve.
The danger which Rodrigo warded off
And the State's safety which his arms restore
Give me alone good grounds for shedding tears.
He's saved the city; he has served the king,
And his brave arm was fatal but to *me*.

THE INFANTA

He has done veritable miracles.

XIMENA

Already this distressing rumour's spread;
I hear him everywhere proclaimed 'as brave
In war as he's unfortunate in love'.

THE INFANTA

How can the people's words distress you so?
This youthful Mars thus praised, he pleased you once.
He was your all in all. He worshipped you;
Vaunting his valour, they endorse your choice.

XIMENA

All with some justice can acclaim his deeds,
But, when I hear him praised, I'm on the rack.
My sorrow grows when he's exalted thus.
I see his loss when I perceive his worth.
Ah! cruel ordeal for a heart in love!
The more his merit's praised, the more I burn.

In spite of that, my duty still prevails,
And, whatsoe'er my love, demands his death.

THE INFANTA

Your duty yesterday won high esteem.
Your self-control appeared so glorious,
So worthy of your will that all at court
Admired your spirit, pitying your love.
But will you take a faithful friend's advice?

XIMENA

Not to obey you would be criminal.

THE INFANTA

What *then* was right's no longer so *today*.
Now Don Rodrigo is our only stay,
The hope and love of an adoring throng,
Castile's support, the terror of the Moor.
The king himself agrees with the belief
Your father lives again in him alone,
And, if in short you wish my frank advice,
Willing his death, you will the State's collapse.
What! to avenge a father, is it right
To hand Spain over to the enemy?
Can your demand be justified for *us*?
Must we share punishment without the crime?
It's not that, after all, you have to wed
The man the dead Count forced you to accuse.
I would myself dissuade you from that course.
Deprive him of your love, but not his life.

XIMENA

Ah! such forgivingness is not for me.
The duty which impels me knows no bounds.
Whate'er my love may say on his behalf –
Adored by all and cherished by the king,
Surrounded by his bravest warriors –
My cypresses will make his laurels fade.

THE INFANTA

It shows great spirit when, to wreak revenge,
Duty attacks someone so dear to us.
But finer still it is to sacrifice
One's blood vendetta to the public weal.
Believe me, you need but withdraw your love.
That will be punishment enough for him.
Accept this measure for the country's good.
In any case, what can the king do now?

XIMENA

He can reject my plea, not silence me.

THE INFANTA

Think well, Ximena, what you wish to do.
Farewell. Alone, at leisure, ponder well.

XIMENA

After my father's death I have no choice.

Scene Three

The king's apartment

DON FERNANDO, DON DIEGO, DON ARIAS,
DON RODRIGO, DON SANCHO

DON FERNANDO

Brave scion of a family renowned,
Which was of old the glory of Castile,
Descendant of such valiant ancestors
Whose gallantry you've equalled from the start,
I cannot fittingly reward your deeds,
And I've less power than you have excellence.
The land delivered from so fierce a foe,
My sceptred hand given new strength by yours,

The Moors undone before, in these alarms,
I had the time to order their repulse,
Are exploits such they hardly leave a king
The means or hope to pay his debt to you.
But your reward comes from two captive kings.
They've named you both in front of me the Cid.
Since in their tongue Cid is as much as lord,
I'll not begrudge you this fair title. Be
Henceforth the Cid. Sweep all before you. Fill
Granada and Toledo with affright,
And let it show to all beneath my sway
Both what you are and what I owe to you.

DON RODRIGO

Sire, condescend to spare my modesty.
You make too much of my slight services,
And I must blush before so great a king,
Not meriting the honour you confer.
I know too well the debt I owe your reign,
The blood that fires me and the air I breathe,
And, when I lose them for so bold an aim,
I only do a subject's duty, Sire.

DON FERNANDO

All those whom service to my duty binds
Do not acquit themselves with that *élan*;
And valour, when it goes not to excess,
Does not produce such rare, unheard-of deeds.
Take then my praise, and of this victory
Recount the tale to me at greater length.

DON RODRIGO

Sire, in this pressing danger, as you know,
Which spread such chilling terror through the town,
A band of friends, met in my father's house,
Incited me, though in a turmoil still . . .
But ah! Sire, pardon my temerity.
I dared to use these men unbid by you.

The peril threatened. They were set to fight.
I risked my head if I appeared at court,
And, if I had to lose it, I preferred
To make my exit fighting in your cause.

DON FERNANDO

I pardon your impetuous revenge.
The State defended speaks in your defence.
Henceforth Ximena will appeal in vain.
I'll hear her only to condole with her.
Say on.

DON RODRIGO

Sire, under me these troops advance,
Bearing themselves with manly confidence.
We started scarce five hundred. Reinforced,
We were, reaching the port, three thousand strong.
To see so many marching, resolute,
Even those who panicked now took heart again.
I hid two thirds of them when we arrived
Deep in the ships we found at anchor there.
The rest whose number constantly increased
Remain around me with impatience fired,
Lie on the ground and, keeping silence, spend
The better part of such a splendid night.
By my command the guard does likewise, and,
Remaining hid, they aid my stratagem.
I boldly feign to have been given by you
The orders which I follow and impart.
This darkling light that from the stars descends
At last shows us the tide with thirty sails.
The waters swell beneath them. Moors and sea,
Moving together, sweep into the port.
We let them pass. Everything seems asleep.
No soldiers in the port; none on the walls.
This silence so profound leads them astray.
Now they are sure they've stolen a march on us.
They heave to, unsuspecting, anchor, land,

And throw themselves into our waiting hands.
Our soldiers rise, and all as if one man,
We rend the welkin with a thousand cries.
Our men echo this clamour from the ships.
They sally forth. The Moors in disarray
Are seized by terror, not yet disembarked.
Before they fight, they deem themselves undone;
They come to pillage and encounter war.
We press them hard on water and on land;
We shed whole rivers of their Moorish blood,
Before they can resist or close their ranks.
But soon their kings despite us rally them;
Morale revives; their terrors are forgot.
The shame of dying without fighting back
Halts the stampede and gives them heart again.
Against us, resolute, they draw their swords,
Mingling our blood most horribly with theirs.
The earth, the river's banks, the fleet, the port,
Are fields of carnage for triumphant death.
How many feats, how many famous deeds
Remain unheralded amid the dark,
In which each man, sole witness of his blows,
Can not discern which way the fates incline!
I scour the field, encouraging our men,
Ord'ring some forward, giving some support,
Directing and inspiring new recruits.
We do not learn the outcome till the dawn.
At last it shows us we have won the day.
The Moor, defeated, sudden loses heart,
And, seeing reinforcements marching up,
The urge to win yields to the fear of death.
Back in their ships, they cut themselves adrift,
And utter to the heavens fearful shrieks
In wild confusion. Now they give no thought
Whether their kings can flee along with them.
The voice of duty's silenced by their fear.
The tide that brought them bears them back again.
Meanwhile, their kings, at grips with our brigade,

With the sore-wounded remnants of their force
Resist courageously, sell their life dear.
I urge them to surrender, but in vain;
Their scimitar in hand, they listen not.
But, at their feet seeing their soldiers fall,
And that henceforth in vain alone they fight,
They ask who is our chief and yield to me.
I sent them both to you together, Sire.
The combat ceased for lack of combatants.
And it was in this way that, serving you . . .

Scene Four

DON FERNANDO, DON DIEGO, DON RODRIGO,
DON ARIAS, DON ALONSO, DON SANCHO

DON ALONSO

Ximena, Sire, comes to ask justice.

DON FERNANDO

Ah!
Annoying news, importunate request!
Go. I'll not force her to set eyes on you.
As all my thanks, I have to drive you out;
But, come, embrace your king before you go.
(*Don Rodrigo goes in.*)

DON DIEGO

Ximena hounds him, but would have him saved.

DON FERNANDO

They say she loves him. I shall test her heart.
Look more depressed.

Scene Five

DON FERNANDO, DON DIEGO, DON ARIAS,
DON SANCHO, DON ALONSO, XIMENA, ELVIRA

DON FERNANDO

At last be satisfied.
The outcome is as you would have it. For,
Although Rodrigo had the upper hand,
He died, as we beheld him, of his wounds.
Give thanks to heaven. You are avenged on him.
(*to Don Diego*)
See how her colour changes suddenly.

DON DIEGO

But see, she swoons. Admire a perfect love
That's manifested in her fainting fit.
Her grief has bared the secrets of her soul,
And suffers you no more to doubt her love.

XIMENA

What! my Rodrigo's dead?

DON FERNANDO

No, no. He lives.
His love for you is still unchangeable.
Allay this overpowering grief for him.

XIMENA

Sire, one can swoon for joy as well as grief.
Excess of pleasure drains our strength away,
And, when it takes our soul, the senses faint.

DON FERNANDO

You wish us to believe what cannot be.
Lady, your grief was plain for all to see.

XIMENA

Well, Sire, then let this be my crowning woe.
Ascribe my fainting to my grieving heart.
My sorrow has reduced me to this point;
His death has robbed me of his guilty head.
If he's expired while fighting for Castile,
Lost is my vengeance and my plans are vain.
So fair an end is too unjust for me.
I want his death, but not a glorious one,
Not with such lustre that it shines on high,
Not on the battlefield, but on the block,
And for my father, not the fatherland.
I want his name bemired, his memory stained.
To die for country's no sad destiny;
That is to live for ever by one's death.
I love, and rightly so, his victory;
It gives me back my victim, saves the State,
But noble, famed, amidst his warriors,
With laurels crowned, instead of victim's wreath,
And, in a word, a worthy sacrifice
To immolate to my dead father's shade . . .
Alas! in what fond hopes do I indulge?
Rodrigo's naught to fear from my revenge.
What can avail my tears against him now?
For him your kingdom is a sanctuary.
There, under you, all is permitted him.
He triumphs over me as o'er his foes;
Justice is stifled in their blood, and serves
As a fresh trophy to the victor's crime.
We swell his glory, and contempt for law
Drags us behind his king-decked chariot.

DON FERNANDO

Daughter, these outbursts are too violent.
Justice must weigh all in the balance. If
The Count was slain, he brought it on himself.
Fairness itself commands me to be mild.
Before accusing me of what I've done,

Consult your heart. Rodrigo lords it there,
And inwardly your love gives thanks to me
For having saved your sweetheart's life for you.

XIMENA

For me! my foe! the object of my wrath!
My sorrow's cause, my father's murderer!
You lay so little store by my demand,
You think t'oblige me by not hearing me.
Since you refuse your justice to my tears,
Permit me, Sire, to have recourse to arms.
It was by arms alone he outraged me;
It is by arms that I must take revenge.
I ask your knights to offer me his head.
Let one of them oblige, and I am his.
Let them, Sire, combat, and, the combat o'er,
I'll wed the victor if Rodrigo falls.
Let this be published, Sire, by your command.

DON FERNANDO

This ancient custom firmly rooted here,
Under the cloak of punishing a slight,
Deprives the State of its best warriors.[1]
Often the grim results of this abuse
Support the guilty, strike the innocent.
Rodrigo is too precious to my throne
Thus to expose him to capricious fate.
Whatever this brave fighter may have done,
The Moors in flight have carried off his crime.

DON DIEGO

What! Sire, for him alone you flout your laws
Which the whole court has seen observed so oft?
What will your people, what will envy say,
If you enable him to save his life,
And give him pretexts to avoid the lists

1. This passage reflects the attempts of the French monarchy to suppress duelling.

Where men of honour seek a glorious death?
Such favours are a blot on your renown.
Let him enjoy his victory unashamed.
The Count was daring. My son punished him
Courageously. He must defend his right.

DON FERNANDO

Since you will have it so, I'll grant your wish.
But, were one slain, hundreds would take his place,
And the prize offered to the victor would
Turn all my knights into his enemies.
To take them on alone would be unfair;
Rodrigo need but once enter the lists.
Choose whom you will, Ximena, and choose well.
After the combat, ask no more of me.

DON DIEGO

Do not excuse those whom his arm astounds.
A field's not open which is barred to all.
After Rodrigo's exploits of today,
What valiant heart would dare to take him on?
Who would against this warrior match himself?
No one so valiant or so rash exists.

DON SANCHO

Throw the field open. The opponent's here.
I am this rash or rather valiant youth.
Grant this one favour to my ardent soul:
Lady, remember what your promise is.

DON FERNANDO

Ximena, you entrust your cause to him?

XIMENA

I've promised.

DON FERNANDO

For tomorrow be prepared.

DON DIEGO

Sire, there is no need for a breathing space.
Preparedness is when morale is high.

DON FERNANDO

To leave the field and fight again at once?

DON DIEGO

He has recovered telling you his deeds.

DON FERNANDO

At least one hour or two I bid him rest.
But, lest this duel form a precedent,
To signify my disapproval of
This gory custom which displeased me so,
Neither my court nor I shall witness it.

(*speaking to Don Arias*)

You'll be sole judge between the combatants.
Be sure both act as men of chivalry.
Bring me the victor when the combat's done.
Whoe'er he is, the same prize goes to him.
I'll give away Ximena, and I'll see
That as reward he will receive her troth.

XIMENA

What! you'll impose so harsh a law on me?

DON FERNANDO

Your love, far from avowing your complaint,
Will gladly take Rodrigo if he wins.
Murmur no more at this unharsh decree;
You'll wed whoever is victorious.

ACT FIVE

Scene One

Ximena's apartment

DON RODRIGO, XIMENA

XIMENA

Rodrigo! You! In daylight! Why so bold?
You'll ruin me. Withdraw, I beg of you.

DON RODRIGO

I mean to die. Lady, I come to you
Before the fatal blow to say farewell.
Th' unalterable love I feel for you
Wishes to make you homage of my death.

XIMENA

You mean to die.

DON RODRIGO

I hasten to the hour
Which will deliver up my life to you.

XIMENA

You'll die. Don Sancho then can strike such fear
Into your heart? He's so redoubtable?
Who has made *you* so weak and *him* so strong?
Rodrigo thinks he's dead before he fights.
Undaunted by my father or the Moors,
He goes to fight Don Sancho in despair.
Thus, then, in direst need, your spirits fail!

DON RODRIGO

I haste not to the fight but to my end.
And, when you seek my death, my ardour quells
All inclination to defend my life.
My mettle is the same, but not my arm
When I preserve a life displeasing you;
And even last night the battle had been lost
Had I been fighting for my cause alone;
But, in defending king and country, I
Would have betrayed them by a poor defence.
My soaring spirit does not hate life so
As to abandon it, forswearing them.
Now that my feelings only are at stake,
I can accept your sentence of my death.
For your revenge, you chose another's hand
(Since I did not deserve to die by yours).
I'll not repulse my adversary's blows;
I must respect them, since he fights for you,
And, happy in the thought they come from you,
Since it's your honour that his arms sustain,
I shall, in fighting him, lay bare my breast,
Revering in his hand your instrument.

XIMENA

If duty's sad, imperious command
Makes me unwillingly demand your death,
And so constrains your love that you must go
Unarmed against whoever fights for me,
Do not, thus blinded, let yourself forget,
Just as your life, your glory is at stake,
And that, whate'er Rodrigo's fame in life,
They'll think him worsted after he is dead.
I love your honour more than *you* love *me*,
Since in my father's blood it dipped your hand
And makes you, too, despite your love renounce
The sweetest hope of making me your own.
But I perceive you rate this hope so low,
That, unresisting, you will court defeat.

What whim destroys your stomach for the fight?
Where is it now, or was it ever there?
Are you so brave only to outrage me?
If you must slight me, does your courage fail?
And will you so besmirch my father's name
That, conquering him, you seek a conqueror?
Do not seek death, but let me sue for it.
Defend your name, even if you scorn to live.

DON RODRIGO

Your father's death and the defeated Moors
Dispense my glory from still further feats.
It can disdain the need for fighting back.
It's known that there is naught I dare not brave,
That everything yields to my sword's attack.
When honour speaks, I care for nothing else.
No, no. Rodrigo in this fight can die
Without the risk of losing his renown,
Without his being charged with cowardice,
Without a victor having vanquished him.
'He loved Ximena,' is what they will say.
'He would not live if he deserved her hate.
He yielded freely to his destiny
Which made his sweetheart clamour for his death.
Had his great heart refused her what she sought,
He would have felt himself a criminal.
Honour revenged lost him his sweetheart's love,
And she, revenged, made him renounce his life,
Preferring still in his enamoured heart,
Honour to his beloved and her to life.'
Thus, in this duel, you will see my death
Enhance my glory, far from dimming it,
And it will follow from my self-willed end,
Since none but I could make you this amend.

XIMENA

Since, to prevent you courting certain death,
Your life and honour have so little weight,

If ever, dear, I loved you, in return,
Fight back to save me from Don Sancho now.
Release me from a grim predicament
Which gives me to a man whom I abhor.
Need I say more? Go, think of your defence,
To force my duty and to silence me;
And, if you love me, come victorious from
A fight for which Ximena is the prize.
Farewell. I blush at having spoken thus.

DON RODRIGO (*alone*)

There is no foe I cannot now subdue.
Come, Navarrese and Moors, Castilians, come,
And all the valiant men that Spain has bred,
Unite together, form an army, try
To fight against a hand thus fortified;
Combine your efforts to destroy my hope,
But still against me you will not prevail.

Scene Two

The Infanta's apartment

THE INFANTA

Shall I still listen to you, pride of birth,
Which brands my passion's flame?
Shall I still list to love whose honeyed words
Against this tyrant make my heart revolt?
Poor princess, to which of the two
Must I do obeisance?
Rodrigo, you are worthy of me now,
But, though you're brave, you're not a monarch's son.

Pitiless fate whose rigour comes between
My rank and my desires!
Can I be sure that, if I choose the Cid,
'Twill cost my passion such keen agony?

O heaven, for how many sighs
Must my poor longing heart prepare,
If after such long torment it can not
Accept the lover or suppress the love.

But this is reasoning too nicely. Why
This deep contempt for such a choice?
Though birth destines my hand to kings alone,
Rodrigo, I with honour can be yours.
After the conquest of two kings,
How could you ever lack a crown?
And this great name of Cid which you have won
Shows clearly you are called upon to reign.

He's worthy of me, but he is not mine.
My gift[1] has worked my harm.
A father's death has stirred so little hate
That she pursues her cause half-heartedly.
Thus, there is nothing to be hoped
From *my* heartache or from *his* crime,
Since destiny to punish me has willed
That love endures between two enemies.

Scene Three

THE INFANTA, LEONORA

THE INFANTA

Why come you, Leonora?

LEONORA

To applaud
The peace of mind that you have found again.

THE INFANTA

Whence could it come when I am deep in woe?

1. Her gift of Rodrigo to Ximena.

LEONORA

If passion feeds on hope, it dies with it.
Rodrigo can no longer charm your heart.
Since, in the combat for Ximena, he
Must either die or else must marry her,
Your hope has faded and your mind's at peace.

THE INFANTA

Ah! far from it!

LEONORA

What can you hope for still?

THE INFANTA

Rather what hope is there that's barred to me?
If on these terms Rodrigo is to fight,
I have too many ways to change its course.
Love, that relentless, that sweet torturer,
To lovers' minds is rich in artifice.

LEONORA

What can you do? Even a father's death
Has not made discord blaze between them. No.
Ximena's conduct makes it all too clear
That her hostility's not caused by hate.
A combat's granted her. And, as her knight,
The first arm offered she accepts at once.
She does not turn to noble, gallant hands
Rendered illustrious by so many feats.
Don Sancho's good enough. She chooses *him*
Because for the first time he takes up arms.
She loves in him his inexperience.
As he is unrenowned, she's unconcerned;
And her facility should make it clear
She seeks a fight which overrules her will,
Offers Rodrigo easy victory
And suffers her at least to seem appeased.

THE INFANTA

I see it well enough, and yet my heart
Vies with Ximena in adoring him.
What must my star-crossed love resolve to do?

LEONORA

To be more mindful of what stock you spring;
You love a subject; heaven owes you a king!

THE INFANTA

The man I worship is no more the same.
I do not love Rodrigo, a mere knight.
My passion calls him by another name;
If I'm in love, it's with a warrior –
The valiant Cid, the master of two kings.
I'll rise above my feelings, not from fear
Of censure but to join two lovers' hearts;
And when, to please me, their devotion's crowned,
I'll not take back the gift that once I made.
Since in this fight his victory is sure,
Let's give him to Ximena once again.
And you who see the wounds that rend my heart,
Behold me finish as I have begun.

Scene Four

Ximena's apartment

XIMENA, ELVIRA

XIMENA

Elvira, pity me. I know not what
To hope for, and I see all's to be feared.
No wish escapes me which I dare approve,
Whate'er I long for, I repent of it.
I call to arms two rivals for my hand;
The happiest outcome will be food for grief.

Whatever fate ordains, this way or that,
My father's unavenged or sweetheart dead.

ELVIRA

This way or that, your agony will end.
You'll have Rodrigo or you'll be avenged.
Whatever destiny ordains, it will
Ensure your glory or a husband.

XIMENA

What!
Or one I hate, or one I rage against!
Rodrigo's or my father's murderer!
In either case, the husband given to me
Is stained with blood of those I cherished most.
In either case, my soul rebels. I fear,
More even than death, the end of this dispute.
Vengeance and love that rack my troubled soul,
You do not tempt me at that fearful price!
And you, O powers above! who torture me,
In this encounter hold the balance even.
Let not the victor win nor vanquished lose.

ELVIRA

That would be treating you too rigorously.
This combat puts you on the rack again,
If after this you still must seek revenge,
Always display this deep resentment, and
Clamour unceasing for Rodrigo's death.
Far better were it for his victory,
Crowning his brow, to silence your demands,
For combat's law to end your sorrows and
The king to make you follow your desires.

XIMENA

If he is victor, think you I will yield?
My duty is too strong, my loss too great.

The law of combat and the king's desire
To overrule them are of no avail.
He can defeat Don Sancho easily,
But not Ximena's glory. Whatsoe'er
A king has promised him on victory,
I will raise up a thousand other foes.

ELVIRA

Beware. To punish overweening pride,
Heaven in the end may grant you your revenge.
What! You will still refuse the happiness
Of being able now to hold your peace
With honour? What can duty hope for? Will
Your sweetheart's death give you your father back?
Is *one* misfortune not enough for you?
Need you pile loss on loss, and grief on grief?
In this caprice with which you are obsessed
You don't deserve the sweetheart destined you,
And we shall see heaven, rightfully incensed,
Leave you Don Sancho when Rodrigo's dead.

XIMENA

Elvira, stop. I am upon the rack.
Do not augment my woe by this presage.
I would prefer not to have either's hand,
But in this fight Rodrigo has my prayers.
Not that my mad love makes me favour him,
But, if he loses, I'm Don Sancho's prize.
This is the fear from which my wishes spring.
But what is this I see? I fear the worst.

Scene Five

DON SANCHO, XIMENA, ELVIRA

DON SANCHO

Forced as I am to bring this sword to you . . .

XIMENA

What! still all dripping with Rodrigo's blood?
Perfidious one! you dare appear to me
Having bereft me of my dearest love?
Break forth, my love, you've nothing more to fear.
My father is avenged! Banish constraint.
This one blow has ensured my good repute,
My soul's despair and my love's liberty.

DON SANCHO

Calm yourself, Lady . . .

XIMENA

You still speak to me,
Murderer of a hero I adore?
You killed him underhand. That gallant knight
Would never have succumbed to such a foe.
You have not served me. Hope for nought from me.
Thinking t'avenge me, you have murdered me.

DON SANCHO

You are mistaken. Far from hearing me . . .

XIMENA

Must I then hear you boasting of his death,
And insolently picturing to my heart
Your valiance, his misfortune and my crime?

Scene Six

The king's apartment

DON FERNANDO, DON DIEGO, DON ARIAS,
DON SANCHO, DON ALONSO, XIMENA, ELVIRA

XIMENA

Sire, there's no need now to dissimulate
What all my efforts could not hide from you.

I loved, but, to avenge a father's death,
I wished a price put on so dear a head.
Your Majesty was witness for yourself
How I made duty triumph over love.
At last, Rodrigo's dead, and I'm transformed
From foe implacable to grieving heart.
I owed this vengeance to my father's shade,
And now I owe my sweetheart these salt tears.
Don Sancho's ruined me defending me.
I'm the reward of his undoing me.
If kings can feel the dint of pity, Sire,
I beg you to revoke your harsh decree.
As prize of such a mournful victory,
I leave him all; let him leave *me* in peace;
Encloistered, let me weep eternally
Father and lover till the day I die.

DON DIEGO

In short, she deems it is no more a crime
To make avowal of her love for him.

DON FERNANDO

Be undeceived! Your sweetheart is not dead.
Don Sancho, vanquished, has misled you.

DON SANCHO

Sire,
She was deceived by her excess of love.
I came to tell the outcome of the fight.
This gallant knight of whom she is entranced,
As he disarmed me, said to me: 'Fear naught.
I'd rather have uncertain victory
Than shed the blood Ximena hazarded.
But, since my duty calls me to the king,
Report the combat to her in my name.
On my behalf, bear her the victor's sword.'
I went to her. This sword deceived her, Sire.
She thought me victor, seeing me return.

Her anger suddenly betrayed her love
With such an outburst of impatience that
I could not win a moment's audience.
Myself, though vanquished, I am fortunate;
And, though my passion's loss is infinite,
I joy in my defeat which has ensured
The happy outcome of a perfect love.

DON FERNANDO (*to Ximena*)

You must not be ashamed of what you feel
Or seek to disavow it, as in vain
Your modesty still urges you to do.
Honour's redeemed and duty is discharged.
Your father's satisfied. He is avenged
By hazarding Rodrigo's life so oft.
You see how heaven disposes differently.
You did all for the Count. Do something for
Yourself. Do not oppose my order which
Gives you a husband you so dearly love.

Scene Seven

DON FERNANDO, DON DIEGO, DON ARIAS,
DON RODRIGO, DON ALONSO, DON SANCHO,
THE INFANTA, XIMENA, LEONORA, ELVIRA

THE INFANTA

Ximena, dry your tears. Gladly receive
This gallant victor from your princess' hand.

DON RODRIGO

Be not offended if, in front of you,
Devotion, Sire, prostrates me at her feet.
I came not here to claim my combat's prize.
I come again to offer you my head.
Lady, my love will not avail itself
Of victory or the wishes of the king.

If everything's too little for revenge,
Say by what means you must be satisfied.
Must I still fight a thousand rivals more,
Show the far marches of the earth my deeds,
Routing an army single-handed and
Eclipsing legendary heroes' fame?
If thus my crime can be at last effaced,
I dare achieve each one of these exploits.
But, if inexorable honour still
Cannot be satisfied without my death,
No longer arm against me others' hands.
Yourself avenge me. Take my proffered head.
You alone vanquish the invincible.
Take vengeance that no other hand can take,
But let my death be punishment enough.
Banish me not from your remembrance and,
Since my demise will keep your glory bright,
As fair return, preserve my memory.
And sometimes say, deploring my sad fate,
'Had he not loved me, he would not be dead.'

XIMENA

Rise. Rise, Rodrigo. I admit it, Sire;
I've said too much for it to be unsaid.
Rodrigo's many virtues speak for him,
And, when a king commands, I must obey.
But whatsoever was your sentence, Sire,
Can you allow this marriage and look on?
And when you call on duty to submit,
Does all your justice harmonize with that?
Rodrigo is a pillar of the State,
But must I be the wages of his deeds?
Must I incur for ever the reproach
Of having hands stained in a father's blood?

DON FERNANDO

Time has repeatedly legitimized
What seemed at first could not be innocent.

Rodrigo won you, and you must be his.
But, though you are the prize of valour, I
Would have to be your glory's enemy
To grant the fruits of victory at once.
Deferment still accords with my decree
Which destines you, at no fixed time, to him.
Take, if you wish, a year to dry your tears.
Rodrigo, meanwhile, will be called to arms.
After, on our own shores, routing the Moors,
Thwarting their plans, repulsing their assaults,
Go, carry war back into Africa,
Command my army, devastate their fields;
At the sole name of Cid, they'll quake with fear.
They've named you lord. They'll want you as their king.
Be faithful to her, though, in all your deeds.
Come back, if possible still worthier
Of her, and rise so high in her esteem
That she will glory then in wedding you.

DON RODRIGO

To win Ximena while I'm serving you,
What can you not bid me accomplish, Sire?
Whatever, absent from her, I endure,
Sire, I go happily and go in hope.

DON FERNANDO

Hope in your courage, in my promise. Hope
Already your belovéd's heart is yours.
And, if her sense of honour still resists,
Leave it to time, your valiance and your king.

END

CINNA

PREFACE

IN *Horatius* and *Cinna* (both dated 1640), Corneille made his return to the theatre after his period of discouragement at the Academy's criticism of *The Cid*. And, for the first time, he looked to Roman history for his subject. His choice of Roman sources was in line with the current trend, and, among Roman themes, conspiracies were particularly in favour, as, for example, Scudéry's *Death of Caesar* (1635) indicates. In putting Cinna's conspiracy against Augustus on the stage, therefore, Corneille was following the fashion which, like most literary modes, was not unconnected with contemporary events – in this case, the rash of plots from which France was suffering at the time. It is fair to add, however, that Corneille borrowed only the central idea of the play from his main source (Seneca, via Montaigne) and a number of other suggestions. The rest is invented.

Corneille refers to Cinna as a tragedy, but it is certainly not tragic by Aristotelian standards. The play, as Adam notes, arouses 'admiration and astonishment' rather than 'pity and terror', and in addition it has the happy ending and optimistic ethos of the tragi-comedy. In fact, like *The Cid*, it is a work glorifying the sublime. And it is only if it is interpreted in this key that we can appreciate the contemporary enthusiasm for the play, and particularly for Emilia, the brain and driving force of the conspirators – 'the fair, the reasonable, the holy and adorable Fury', as one admirer called her.

For, at first blush, the subject is hardly calculated to appeal to a modern audience. The action takes place at three levels, none of which can be easily transposed into up-to-date terms. First, there is the battle in the mind of Augustus (indicated by the sub-title *The Clemency of Augustus*) as to whether to pardon Cinna and the other plotters or kill them. There is the debate between the supporters of absolute rule (in this case, by Augustus) and the partisans of liberty. And lastly, behind and largely conterminous with this second group, is a series of personal reasons motivating the conspirators.

The arguments for and against clemency on the part of a ruler were vigorously debated under Louis XIII. Cardinal Richelieu, the King's prime minister, was beginning to transform a feudal system into a centralizing monarchy, a process which was to be carried very much further under Louis XIV. Conspiracies by the great lords were the order of the day; there were at least a dozen under Richelieu alone. When it came to dealing with the lesser orders, as the ruthless repression of the rising around Corneille's native Rouen in 1639 showed, the Cardinal did not stand on ceremony. But, when it came to dealing with the notables, the problem was somewhat different. The current view was that the King's function was to mete out justice to the various estates, but to be merciful and indulgent to the key nobles who were regarded as coming only slightly below the monarch. This Christian philosophy regarded society as an organic combination of interlinking parts and took an optimistic view of human nature. But the opposite school, based on Machiavelli, was making headway, encouraged by Richelieu.[1] This tendency considered the state from a strictly rational and functional point of view and regarded violence, ruse and treachery as useful instruments for strengthening government.

With consummate skill and inventiveness, Corneille shows us both sides of the coin – the servitude and greatness of a dictator. Nevertheless, he comes down strongly on the side of absolute rule. To start with, it is true, we see the emperor through the eyes of his opponents, who dwell on the rivers of blood through which he has waded to the throne and on his suppression of the ancient Roman liberties. But, as the play gathers momentum, the perspective changes. Augustus, we realize, is fully conscious of the burden of guilt weighing on him and of the constant and understandable hatred of his rule. He is ready to step down from his anguish-laden throne, and is only prevented from doing so by Cinna's disingenuous

1. 'Richelieu . . . a great-hearted [*généreux*] friend, a cruel enemy, kept on the same table his breviary and Machiavelli.' (The abbé de Choisy)

pleas. When the conspirators are discovered, Augustus grows rapidly in stature. He reduces Cinna to silence and confusion by recalling the favours heaped on him and ridicules the aims of the plotters by laying bare the weakness of their 'platform'. They have nothing, he points out, to put in his place and would in any case be swept aside by the great patrician families immediately on seizing power. But it is when, in a final burst of sublimity, he pardons Cinna that the dramatist comes out entirely in favour of the emperor. Nor is this an accident. For, in this grandiose gesture, Corneille tempers his approval of absolutism with the liberal conception of monarchy defended by the feudal, romanesque ethos. A modern spectator may remain unmoved by such nobility of mind, but it was precisely this trait which elicited wild applause from the audiences of his day.

In the same way, when Emilia renounces violence and is converted to accepting Augustus' rule, this is not because, as Adam notes, she brings into play some theoretical mechanism of will-power, but because she acts by *élans* or sublime impulses and lives in an atmosphere of grandeur. If we find her sudden change of stance unconvincing, this is for the same reasons that Augustus' forgiveness of Cinna fails to strike a chord in us. We tend to equate such nobility of soul with bombast. Yet, as contemporaries such as Guez de Balzac emphasized, the essence of the Roman spirit, for Corneille, was gravity, sobriety and resoluteness.

When we come to the second stratum of the issues debated in *Cinna*, we are on more familiar ground. This is the clash between a liberal tradition (however vaguely defined) and a dictatorship (whose arbitrariness and crimes, however, are placed in the past when the subsequently absolute ruler was still consolidating his hold). Moreover, as already noted, the libertarians have a purely negative aim – to end the dictatorship. There is not a word in the play about how they will rule the unmanageable empire which was proving a strain on the indefatigable and able Augustus. The issue, in fact, is largely a fictitious one which is good as a theme for several impassioned speeches and as a means of whipping up the enthusiasm of the conspirators. But the fight is not really between the present evils of absolutism and the positive ideals of the opposition.

Indeed, when we examine (the third stratum) the motives of the plotters, we find that these are mostly extraneous to the question of freedom. Cinna, the leader, is driven on by love. Many of the others, as Augustus cuttingly observes, are good-for-nothings up to their ears in debt, whose only hope of survival is a general upheaval. Significantly, the one genuine 'freedom-fighter' is the wavering and despicable Maximus, but even he betrays the cause out of jealousy. In stressing these aspects of the conspiracy, Corneille, without bringing in specific references to any particular contemporary plot, has given a convincing picture of the 'futility of the motives, the abuse of the high-falutin' formulas, the indiscretions, the imprudences, and above all the role played by love in these undertakings which it was bound to compromise'.

Cinna, then, suggests that Corneille had, since *The Cid*, moved some way towards accepting Richelieu's efforts to strengthen the monarchy as a centralizing force. Certainly it is not surprising that the play (like *Horatius*) met with the all-powerful Cardinal's enthusiastic approval.

A similar shift is visible on the technical level. The work has the streamlined, fast-moving compactness (and even almost complete observance of the unities) pointing forward to Racine's tragedies (which run parallel to Louis XIV's absolute monarchy). The action hinges on psychological decisions, which enables Corneille to achieve a degree of dramatic concentration rarely attained by him in any other work. There are no purely oratorical frills; the action moves smoothly and rapidly forward after a perfect exposition (if we except the horrendously involved six opening lines), suspense is superbly maintained and the audience kept on tenterhooks right up to the final decision of Augustus. The fifth act is as powerful as the others, whereas in, for example, *Horatius*, Corneille had tended to show signs of flagging towards the end. The verse, hard-hitting and incisive, has remarkable resonance and power. If, as certain critics have maintained, Corneille took the wrong turning after *The Cid*, the very least that can be said is that the change yielded a political masterpiece.

CINNA SUMMARY

ACT ONE

In a monologue Emilia expresses her concern at the danger which Cinna, her beloved, is exposed to because he has agreed at her instigation to plot the murder of Augustus, who had caused her father's death. Cinna, who has come from the final deliberations of the conspirators, informs Emilia that the plotters are ready to strike. Augustus sends for Cinna and Maximus (the other leader of the plot), and Emilia fears that everything has been discovered.

ACT TWO

But, in fact, what has happened is that Augustus, weary of the cares of office and of the constant threats to his life, is ready to abdicate. However, he first wishes to consult his two most trusted advisers. Maximus urges Augustus to renounce the throne. Cinna, on the contrary, realizing that Emilia's vengeance is lost if Augustus is no longer emperor, urges him to stay in power. Augustus decides in Cinna's favour. But, in continuing to rule Rome, he adds new favours to those already heaped on the two men. Cinna is given Emilia's hand. Maximus begins to suspect the jealously guarded secret of the mutual love of Cinna and Emilia.

ACT THREE

In the opening scene, the audience learns that Cinna has told Maximus everything – including the part played by Emilia in inspiring the conspiracy. Maximus, who is in love with Emilia, now finds that he is really serving the cause of his rival rather than that of Rome. His confidant, Euphorbus, advises Maximus to reveal the plot to Augustus and thereby ruin Cinna and win Emilia. Maximus hesitates. Cinna confesses to him that he is reluctant to go on with the conspiracy in view of Augustus' generosity to him. Maximus urges him to be true to his oath to avenge Roman freedom. Cinna debates within himself whether to go on or draw back, and decides to try to persuade Emilia to release him from his oath to serve her revenge. But, when he appeals to his beloved to do so, she launches at him a volley of withering contempt. Cinna sees that there is no way out, but swears that, after the assassination, he will take his own life. Emilia is distraught, but refuses to alter her plans.

ACT FOUR

Euphorbus, authorized by his master, informs Augustus of the plot, accuses Cinna of being the ringleader, and portrays the others as reluctant accomplices. Augustus indulges in a long monologue in which he wavers between clemency and repression. Livia, the empress, throws her weight on the side of leniency. Emilia learns that Cinna has been sent for again by Augustus and that Maximus has disappeared. She assumes that all is lost, and prepares to take her life. Maximus, who has himself put out the false report of his suicide, appeals to Emilia to flee with him, and declares his love. He is haughtily rejected, and goes off in despair, putting all the blame for the failure of his intrigues on Euphorbus.

ACT FIVE

Augustus reminds Cinna of the endless favours received from his hand. He humiliates his opponent by proving that Cinna can offer no valid alternative to Augustus' own rule. Cinna is summoned to choose the form of death he prefers. Emilia and Livia come on the scene, and Augustus learns that Emilia, whom he treated as a daughter, is the soul of the conspiracy and that Cinna has acted merely out of love for her. Cinna seeks to defend her and claims that he had planned the murder before falling in love with her. Both lovers demand to be put to death. Maximus confesses the truth about his own role. Augustus is overwhelmed by this torrent of devastating revelations. In the end, summoning up his greatness of soul, he pardons everyone. Emilia is finally converted to belief in the rule of Augustus, and Livia prophesies that there will be no further attempts on Augustus' life and that he will go down to posterity as a model ruler.

DEDICATION
TO MONSIEUR DE MONTAURON[1]

(1643)

Monsieur,

I present to you a picture of one of the finest acts of Augustus. This monarch was completely open-hearted[2] and open-handed,[2] and his generosity never appeared with such lustre as in the seeds of his clemency and his liberality. These two rare virtues came so naturally to him and were so inseparable in him that it seems that, in this story which I have set on our stage, they stimulated each other in his soul. He had been so liberal towards Cinna that, the latter's conspiracy having revealed an extraordinary ingratitude, he needed an extraordinary effort of clemency to pardon him. And the pardon which he gave him was the source of new favours which he lavished on him to win over a heart which had not been fully conquered by the first favours. So that it is true to say that Augustus would have been less clement towards Cinna if he had been less liberal, and that he would have been less liberal had he been less clement. That being so, to whom could I more fittingly dedicate the portrait of one of these heroic virtues than to him who possesses the other in so high a degree, since, in this act, this great prince so closely linked and (so to speak) united one to the other? You have riches, but you know how to enjoy them, and you enjoy them in so noble, so distinguished and so illustrious a manner that you compel the public voice to confess that fortune consulted reason when it bestowed its favours on you, and one has more cause to wish these to be doubled than to envy their abundance. I have lived so remote from flattery that I think I am entitled to be believed when I speak well of someone; and,

1. A rich financier who was lavish in his patronage of the arts.
2. 'Généreux', in the original.

when I accord praise (which happens fairly rarely), it is with so much restraint that I always suppress a host of glorious truths, so as not to incur the suspicion that I flaunt obliging lies which so many people these days are expert at retailing so glibly. Hence, I shall say nothing of the advantages of your birth, or of your courage which has so worthily sustained you in the profession of arms in which you spent your early years. These things are too well known by everyone. I shall say nothing of the prompt and powerful assistance which is daily given to so many estimable families ruined by the disorders of our wars. These are things which you would like to keep concealed. I shall say only a word about the particular quality which you have in common with Augustus. It is that this generosity which composes the better part of your soul and reigns over the other, and which can be rightly termed the soul of your soul, since it is the driving force of all its powers, it is that, I repeat, this generosity, following the example of that great emperor, takes pleasure in extending itself to men of letters, in an age when too many think that they have sufficiently rewarded literary works when they have honoured them with sterile praise. And certainly you have treated some of our muses so bountifully that in them you have obliged all the others, so that there are none who do not owe you thanks. Please, Monsieur, allow me to acquit myself of all that I recognize I owe you by presenting you with this poem, which I have chosen as the most lasting of my works to inform those who will read it in the future that Monsieur de Montauron, by liberality unheard-of in the present century, has placed all the muses under an obligation to him, and that I am so appreciative of the benefits with which you have astonished some of them that all my life I shall call myself,

Monsieur,

Your very humble and very devoted servant,

CORNEILLE

CAST

OCTAVIUS-CAESAR AUGUSTUS, *Emperor of Rome*

LIVIA, *the Empress*

CINNA, *son of a daughter of Pompey the Great, and leader of the conspiracy against Augustus*

MAXIMUS, *the other leader of the conspiracy*

EMILIA, *daughter of Augustus' tutor, C. Toranius, who was proscribed by Augustus during the triumvirate*

FULVIA, *Emilia's confidante*

POLYCLETES, *a freedman of Augustus*

EVANDER, *a freedman of Cinna*

EUPHORBUS, *a freedman of Maximus*

The scene is at Rome

CINNA
OR
THE CLEMENCY OF AUGUSTUS

ACT ONE

Scene One

Emilia's apartment

EMILIA[1]

Impatience for illustrious revenge
To which my father's death[2] has given rise,
My fierce resentment's headstrong child, which I
Blindly embrace, by sorrow led astray,
Your tyranny is all too powerful.
For a few moments grant me respite, and
Let me consider at the present point
Both what I risk and what I undertake.[3]
When I behold Augustus throned on high
And you remind my grieving memory
That, by his hand, my father massacred
Was the first stepping-stone to that same throne,
When you present to me this blood-stained scene –
My hatred's cause, his raging wrath's effect –
I give myself entirely up to you;
For this one death, a thousand deaths are due.
And yet, although by fury overcome,
I love my Cinna more than I hate *him*,
And I can feel this fiery anger cool
When it involves exposing my beloved.

1. Emilia comes on stage after the curtain has risen.
2. Emilia's father, C. Toranius, had been put to death by Augustus.
3. She risks sending Cinna to his death by what she undertakes, which is to have Augustus murdered.

Yes, Cinna, I am angry with myself,
Thinking of all the risks I make you run.
You serve me fearlessly, but, asking you
For Caesar's life, I must expose your own.
Nor do exalted heads roll in the sand
Without a fearful whirlwind being sown;
The outcome's doubtful and the peril's sure.
A faithless friend can give away the plot;
A bungled plan, a chance not promptly seized,
Can cause the venture to recoil on you,
Who will receive the blows you aimed at him;
It can envelop you in its collapse;
And can, despite the efforts of your love,
In falling, Cinna, crush you under it.
Ah! cease to run this mortal danger, for
Revenge which loses you is no revenge.
It is a cruel heart which can delight
In joy that's marred by bitterness, and we
Must reckon as a crowning ill a foe's
Destruction if it costs so many tears.
But are there tears when fathers are avenged?
Are not all losses light at such a price?
And, when the murderer falls beneath our blow,
Must we consider what his death has cost?
Cease then, vain terrors, craven tenderness,
To let your weakness undermine my heart;
And you who breed them by your vain concern,
Love, serve my duty, far from fighting it.
Defeat by it is glorious! Victory
Is shameful. Let it overcome you now.
Duty will pay you back a thousandfold;
And it will triumph but to crown your love.

Scene Two

EMILIA, FULVIA

EMILIA

I've sworn it, Fulvia, and I swear again,
Though loving Cinna, if I'm to be his,
Augustus first must perish; and his head
Is the sole price at which I'm to be won.
These are the terms duty dictates to me.

FULVIA

These are too fair for me to criticize.
This grand design merely confirms you as
The daughter of the man you would avenge;
But, once again, allow me to suggest
You would do well to let your ardour cool.
Each day Augustus by his bounteousness
Seems to repay the evil he has done;
His favour to you is so manifest
And in his palace you are so esteemed
That often his most smiled-on courtiers
Beg you on bended knee to plead their cause.

EMILIA

All this can never bring my father back;
And, in whatever light you look at me,
My wealth unbounded, influence immense,
Fulvia, I'm a proscript's daughter still.
Benefits need not make for gratitude;
Given by a hand that's hated, they offend.
The more we heap them on potential foes,
The more we give them arms for treachery.
His daily favours leave my heart unchanged;
I'm as I was, but much more powerful,
And, with the gifts he pours into my hands,

CINNA

I buy, to fight him, Roman consciences;
I would accept even Livia's place from him
If that would help my hand to strike him down.
There are no crimes when fathers are avenged;
Favours can not buy filial loyalty.

FULVIA

What need, though, to be thought ungrateful. Why
Can you not hate without displaying it?
So many others have not yet forgot
Upon what cruelties the throne was built.
So many Romans, brave, illustrious men,
Victims of his ambitions and his crimes,
Leave to their children sorrows that ensure
That they'll avenge *your* loss in *their* revenge.
Many have tried. Thousands will follow them.
Who lives hated by all can not live long.
Place in their hands our common interests,
And aid their plans only by secret prayers.

EMILIA

What! Hate him and not try to do him ill?
Leave it to chance to bring about his doom?
And satisfy such urgent duties by
An òbscure hate and ineffectual prayers?
His wished-for downfall would be gall to me,
If he for others than my father fell;
And you would see my tears flow for his death
If it deprived me of my just revenge.
It's cowardice to look to others for
The public interests which converge with ours.
Let us combine the sweetness of revenge
With glory won by striking tyrants down,
And let us publish throughout Italy:
'Rome's freedom is Emilia's doing, for
Her soul was touched, her heart enamoured, but
Only at such a price she gave her love.'

FULVIA

Love at that price is but a poisoned gift
And clearly spells your lover's downfall. But
Emilia, think what you expose him to.
How many men have foundered on this reef;
Blind not yourself. His fate is plain to all.

EMILIA

Ah! you have struck me at my weakest point.
When I recall the risks I make him run,
Fear of his death already makes me die;
My mind in turmoil wars within itself.
I wish and do not wish, dare and draw back.
And duty, in confusion, listless, stunned,
Yields to the urge of my rebellious heart.
But, soft, my passion, hold yourself in check;
You see how great the risk. No matter though.
Cinna's not doomed because exposed to it.
Whatever legions guard Augustus and
Whatever his precautions and his plans,
To scorn one's life is to be lord of it.
A greater peril bears a sweeter fruit;
Heroism commands it, glory follows it.
But, whether Cinna or Augustus dies,
This sacrifice I owe my father's shade.
That Cinna vowed when he received my troth;
For that alone he's worthy of my love.
Now is too late for going back on it.
Today we meet, today the plot is hatched;
The hour, the place, the hand will be arranged,
And after that all we can do is die.

Scene Three

CINNA, EMILIA, FULVIA

EMILIA

But here he comes. Cinna, did not the fear
Of danger cloud your meeting's harmony?
And from your friends' reactions can you see
Whether they're ready to keep faith with you?

CINNA

Never did enterprise conceived against
A tyrant give such promise of success;
Never so firmly did they swear his death.
Conspirators were never more at one;
They all aspire to it with so much joy,
They seem like me to serve the one they love;
All burn with such an angry fire, they seem
Like you to seek a father's dear revenge.

EMILIA

I had foreseen that for this enterprise
Cinna would choose none but the valiantest,
And would not place in undistinguished hands
The interests of Emilia and of Rome.

CINNA

Would you had seen yourself how zealously
This band so fair a venture undertakes!
At the sole name of Caesar Emperor,
You would have seen their eyes inflamed with rage,
And in one moment by conflicting signs
Turn pale with horror and with fury red.
'Friends, the auspicious day is here,' I said,
'Which will at last conclude our noble plans.
Heaven in our hand has placed the fate of Rome,

And its salvation hangs on one man's doom,
If this non-human can be called a man,
This tiger ravenous for Roman blood.
To shed this blood how oft has he intrigued!
How often has he changed faction and side,
Now friend of Antony, and now his foe,
And never fierce or insolent by halves.'
There, by a long account of all the woes
Inflicted in our childhood on our sires,
Fanning their hatred with the memory,
I fired their eagerness to punish him.
The ill-starred battles first I conjured up,
In which Rome by his hands was disembowelled,
When eagle struck down eagle; on each side
Our legions armed to crush their liberty;
When the best soldiers and the bravest chiefs
Placed their main glory in becoming slaves;
When, to ensure their shameful servitude,
They sought to bind to them the universe;
And when the execrable lust for power
Made the foul name of traitor loved by all.
Romans with Romans, brothers 'mongst themselves,
Fought to decide which tyrant was to rule.
I drew a fearful picture of their reign,
Unholy, hideous, unmerciful,
Fatal to all good men, the senate and
The rich, in short of the triumvirate.[1]
But I could find no colours dark enough
To represent its tales of tragedy.
I showed them vying with each other in
Murder, all Rome drowned in her children's blood,
Some done to death even in the public squares,
The others clinging to their household gods,
The wicked by rewards driven on to crime,
The husband by the wife slain in his bed,
The son all dripping with his father's blood

1. 'The triumvirate' was formed by Octavius (as Augustus was formerly known), Antony and Lepidus.

Demand his wages for the severed head.
But all these gruesome traits could not express
More than a fraction of their blood-stained peace.
Shall I repeat the names of these great men,
Whose murder I described to fire their hate,
The famous proscripts, mortal demigods,
Sacrificed on the very altar steps?
Would I could tell you to what pitch of rage,
To what deep shudders, to what violence
These shameful deaths, although so poorly limned,
Inflamed the minds of the conspirators.
I lost no time. Seeing them so enraged,
Blind to all fear, ready for anything,
I briefly added: 'All these cruelties,
The loss of all our goods and liberties,
The country ravaged and the pillaged towns,
And the proscriptions and the civil wars,
These are the blood-stained steps that took him up
To Caesar's throne, from which he governs us.
But we can change this ghastly destiny,
Since of three tyrants one alone remains;
The only time that he forewent support
Was when he ruined two[1] to reign alone.
No master can replace him. Once he's dead,
With liberty, Rome will be born again,
And we'll deserve the name of Romans if
We smash the yoke that bears so hard on her.
The moment is propitious. Let us strike.
Tomorrow on the Capitol he makes
A sacrifice. Let that be *him*, and there
Let us before the gods see justice done.
Our men compose most of his retinue;
He will receive the incense from my hand,
And, at the signal, this same hand will place
No incense but a dagger in his heart.
Thus, by a deadly blow the victim felled

1. Antony was killed, and Lepidus excluded from the triumvirate.

Will show whether I am of Pompey's[1] blood.
Show, after me, whether you're mindful of
The glorious ancestors from which you spring.'
Scarce had I finished when each one renewed
By solemn oath the vow of loyalty.
They liked the plan, but each one claimed the right
To strike the blow I had assigned myself.
Reason at last made their excitement cool.
Maximus and one half will seize the door;
The rest will follow, and will be prepared
To ring him[2] round at a quick word from me.
There, fair Emilia, then, is where we stand.
Tomorrow I await applause or hate,
A liberator's name or parricide's,
And Caesar a usurper's or a king's.
The outcome of our fight with tyranny
Will bring us ignominy or renown;
And the plebs, fickle towards all tyrants, if
It hates them dead adores them when alive.
For me, whether heaven smiles or frowns on me,
Lifts me to glory or consigns to death,
And Rome for or against us shows her hand,
Dying for you, all will seem sweet to me.

EMILIA

Fear not an outcome which will soil your fame.
If good or bad, your glory is undimmed;
In such an enterprise, ill-fortune will
Endanger not your honour but your life.
Consider Cassius' fate and Brutus's.
Did it obscure the splendour of their name?
Are they, their grand designs, completely dead?
Are they now counted as the dregs of Rome?
No, no. Their memory is dear to all
As much as Caesar's life is odious;

1. Pompey the Great (Cnaeus Pompeius Magnus, 106–48 BC), member of the First Triumvirate.

2. Augustus.

CINNA

He won the day, but Romans mourn for them,
And all their like wish they were back again.
Go, follow in their steps where honour calls.
But do not be neglectful of your life;
Remember the bright ardour of our love.
As well as fame *I* shall be your reward.
Your heart is mine, my favours will be yours;
Your life is precious, mine depends on it.
But what can bring Evander hither?

Scene Four

CINNA, EMILIA, EVANDER, FULVIA

EVANDER

Sir,
Caesar has sent for you and Maximus.

CINNA

Both Maximus and me? But are you sure?

EVANDER

Polycletes awaits you at your house,
And would himself have come to look for you
Had I not skilfully prevented him.
I warn you, Sir, in case of a surprise.
Action is urgent.

EMILIA

Send for both the chiefs
At the same time! You are discovered.

CINNA

God!
Let us hope not.

EMILIA

Cinna, I'll be your death;
And the gods, bent on shielding tyranny,
Have slipped some traitor in among your friends.
There is no doubt, Augustus has learned all.
What! both, the moment that the die was cast?

CINNA

I cannot hide from you that I am stunned,
But I am often summoned to his side.
Maximus is, like me, a trusted friend.
We are perhaps alarmed without due cause.

EMILIA

Be at less trouble to deceive yourself.
Drive me not, Cinna, to the breaking point.
Since from now on you can avenge me not,
At least from this dire peril save yourself.
Flee from Augustus' unrelenting wrath;
My father's death has cost me tears enough.
Do not inflict fresh torment on my grief,
Reducing me to mourn the man I love.

CINNA

What! you allow yourself to panic and
Betray your interest and the public weal!
This shows a lack of confidence in me.
You give up all when we must hazard all.
What will our friends not do if you are wrong?

EMILIA

If the plot's known, what will become of you?

CINNA

If to betray me there are minds so low,
My constancy at least will never quail.
You'll see it on the verge of the abyss,

CINNA

Blazing with glory, dare the torturer,
Make Caesar jealous of the blood he'll shed,
Force him to tremble when he seeks my doom.
I shall be suspect if I tarry here.
Farewell. Revive your noble spirits. If
I have to bear the blows of destiny,
I shall both happy and unhappy die –
Happy in serving you to lose my life,
Unhappy unavailingly to die.

EMILIA

Yes, go and disregard my pleas to stay.
My turmoil is dispelled, my reason stirs.
Forgive, my love, these shameful weaknesses.
Cinna, you would in vain seek to escape.
If all's discovered, Caesar has made sure
That it's no longer in your power to flee.
Bear, bear to him this manly confidence,
Worthy both of our love and of your birth;
Die, if you must, a citizen of Rome,
And by a great death crown a great design.
Fear not when you are gone that I'll live on.
Your death will carry off my soul towards yours.
And, pierced at once by the same blows, my heart . . .

CINNA

Dead as I'll be, let me still live for you,
And, dying, suffer me at least to hope
That you'll avenge father and lover too.
You've naught to fear. None of our friends has learned
Either your plans or promises to me.
I spoke just now of Rome's sad plight, but I
Was silent on the death[1] that caused our hate,
Lest my enthusiasm on your behalf
Revealed the secret of our love. Alone
Fulvia and Evander know of it.

1. That of Emilia's father.

EMILIA

I'll go to Livia's then with less affright,
Since, in your peril, there remains a way
Of using both her influence and mine.
But, if my love can not deliver you,
Do not expect me to live after you.
Your destiny will now decide my fate,
I shall obtain your life, or die with you.

CINNA

I beg you, be less cruel to yourself.

EMILIA

Go, and recall only my love for you.

ACT TWO

Scene One

Augustus' private apartment

AUGUSTUS, CINNA, MAXIMUS, TROOP OF COURTIERS

AUGUSTUS

Let all withdraw and no one enter here.
You, Cinna, stay and you, Maximus, too.

(*All withdraw except Cinna and Maximus*)

This empire absolute on land and sea,
This sov'reignty over the universe,
This boundless greatness, this illustrious rank
Which by such toil and blood was earned for me,
In short, all that in my good fortune is adored
By tedious and flattering courtiers,
Is but a glamorous beauty such as those
One loves no more as soon as they're enjoyed.
Ambition when it's sated turns to gall,
Its ardour followed by its opposite;
And, as our mind, until the day we die,
Aspiring always to some fixèd goal,
With no firm hold falls back upon itself,
And at the summit longs but to descend.
I wished for power and I achieved it, but
I did not know it when I wished for it.
I found, possessing it, its only joy
Was ghastly cares, perpetual alarms,
Unnumbered foes and death at every turn,
No pleasure unalloyed or peace of mind.
Before me, Sulla wielded power supreme.
Caesar the great, my father, held it too,

But each took such a different view of it,
One gave it up, the other clung to it.
The one, cruel and barbarous, died at peace,
Beloved, like a good citizen, at home;
The other, though a gentle, friendly man,
Was cut down basely in the senate-house.
These yesterday's examples would suffice
If by example only were we led.
One beckons me to follow, one appals;
But oft examples are deceptive, and
Destiny's plan which weighs on mortal thoughts
Not always in things past is charactered.
Sometimes one founders, and the other's saved.
And one survives by what another's killed.
That, my dear friends, is what is troubling me.
You fill Agrippa's and Maecenas' place.
To solve this problem I discussed with them,
Assume the power they exercised on me,
And disregard this majesty supreme;
Odious to Rome, oppressive to myself.
Treat me as friend, and not as sovereign.
Augustus, Rome, the State are in your hands;
You'll place all Europe, Asia,[1] Africa,
Under a monarch's or republic's rule.
Your word is law for me, and it alone
Makes me an emperor or a citizen.

CINNA

In spite of our surprise and my poor skill,
I shall obey you without flattery.
I'll lay aside inhibiting respect,
And fight the view to which you seem inclined.
Allow me in my zeal for your renown
To say that you would leave a stain on it
If you approved these promptings to the point
Of passing judgement on your previous acts.
One does not give up lawful sovereignty.

1. Asia Minor.

What's cost no crime is kept without remorse.
The more what's given up is of great prize,
The more who dares to give it up condemns
It as ill-gotten. Do not brand, my lord,
Those rarest virtues which have made you king.
Power is yours justly, not by *coup d'état;*
You have but changed the form of government.
Rome is beneath your rule by right of war,
Which under Roman rule has placed the world;
Your arms have conquered it, and conquerors
Are never tyrants though usurping power;
When they by force have subjugated states,
Governing justly, they are justly kings.
That is what Caesar did. And you must now
Condemn his policy or do like him.
If for Augustus total power was wrong,
Then Caesar was a tyrant rightly killed,
And you must give account for all the blood
Shed to avenge him and ascend the throne.
You must not fear the evil destinies;
A stronger genius watches over you.
Ten times attempts upon your life have failed;
Those bent on killing Caesar struck at once.
There's many a scheme, but oft they go awry.
There are assassins but no Brutus yet.
In short, if such a dire reverse must be,
How fine to die lord of the universe.
This is what briefly I make bold to say,
And Maximus, I'm sure, agrees with me.

MAXIMUS

I grant Augustus has the right to keep
The sway his qualities alone have won;
Shedding his blood, imperilling his life,
He has made lawful conquest of the State.
But that he cannot without shame lay down
The burden he is tired of carrying,
That he indicts Caesar of tyranny,

And ratifies his death, *that* I deny.
All Rome is yours, dominion of it too.
Each has the free disposal of what's his.
He can at will keep or get rid of it.
Why cannot you alone do like the plebs?
Must you, having subdued the world, become
Slave of the greatness you have risen to?
Possess them without their possessing you;
Let them not master you but do your will.
Let it in short be trumpeted abroad
That all they offer is beneath you, Sir.
Your Rome once gave you birth, and now you wish
To give it your omnipotence. And yet
Cinna regards it as a deadly sin
To be so liberal to your native Rome!
He calls remorse love of the fatherland!
By lofty virtue, glory is besmirched,
And it is but an object of contempt
And reaps dishonour if it abdicates.
I readily admit that such an act
Gives Rome much more than you've received from it.
But is the crime unpardonable when
The gratitude is greater than the gift?
Follow, my lord, the heavens inspiring you.
Your star shines brighter when despising power;
And you'll go down to far posterity
Much less for winning than for leaving it.
Mere luck can lead to sovereignty, my lord,
But leaving it's unheard-of selflessness,
And few will go so far as to disdain
The joys of empire when they've conquered it.
Recall, moreover, that you reign in *Rome*.
Whatever name your court may call you by,
They hate the monarchy, and 'emperor'
Concealing 'king' horrifies Rome no less.
For them a master is a tyrant, Sir;
Who serves him is a traitor and a slave,
Who suffers him is spineless, cowardly,

And any move for freedom is extolled.
The proofs of this are irrefutable.
Ten vain attempts were made upon your life.
Perhaps the next is ready to be launched,
And this same prompting that inspires you now
Is but a secret signal sent from heaven
Which has no other means of saving you.
Expose yourself no longer to these blows.
It's fine to die lord of the universe,
But even the finest death's no epitaph
When we could have, alive, increased our fame.

CINNA

If love of fatherland must here prevail,
It is its welfare only you must seek;
This freedom which appears so dear to it
For Rome is an imaginary prize.
It does more harm than good; it comes not near
What a good monarch offers to the state.
He allocates honours discerningly,
Meting out fit rewards and punishments,
And, as a rightful owner, sees to all
Unpressed by fear of a successor.[1] But
The people's rule is one long uproar where
The voice of reason never can be heard;
Honours are sold to those who covet them,
And power ends in disaffected hands.
These petty sovereigns whom the people choose
For one brief year, seeing their power so short,
Pick, still unripe, the fruit of wisest plans
For fear they leave it to their afterlords.
Their stake is tiny in the common weal;
They reap wide swathes, then, in the public field,
Certain that each will pardon them, since he
Expects the same indulgence in his turn.
The worst of states, Sir, is the people's state.

1. Alludes to the consuls, whose term of office was for one year.

AUGUSTUS

Yet it's the only one that thrives in Rome.
This hate of kings for half a thousand years,[1]
Fed to the children at their mother's breast,
Is too ingrained for us to extirpate.

MAXIMUS

Yes, to its sickness Rome is too attached;
Its people joy in it and flee the cure.
The custom and not reason wins the day;
And this old error Cinna would destroy
Is a most happy one which he adores
By which the world, under the people's yoke,
Has seen it[2] tread on many royal heads,
Its treasures swollen by pillaged provinces.
What more could even the best of kings give Rome?
I would affirm, my lord, that in all climes
All types of State are not acceptable.
Each state conforms to people's character,
And, without wronging that, can not be changed.
Such is the law of heaven whose equity
Strews this diversity throughout the world.
The Macedonians love their monarchy;
And other Greeks more public liberty;
Parthians and Persians opt for sovereigns, but
For Rome the consulate alone is right.

CINNA

It's true that heaven's foresight infinite
Allots a different genius to each race;
But none the less this heaven-dictated plan
Is modified by time as well as place.
Rome from its kings at birth received its walls;
Its consuls gave it power and renown.
It now receives from your rare graciousness

1. Since the expulsion of the Tarquins in 509 BC
2. The people.

Its crowning boon, sovereign prosperity.
The state's no longer pillaged by the troops;
The gates of Janus by your hands are closed.[1]
This feat its consuls only once achieved,
And only, too, the second of its kings.

MAXIMUS

All changes in the state decreed by heaven
Are bloodless and are not death's harbingers.

CINNA

It is the gods' design unfailingly
To sell us somewhat dear their benefits.
Even the Tarquins' exile drenched our land
With blood, and our first consuls cost us wars.

MAXIMUS

Your grandsire, Pompey, then resisted heaven
In fighting to defend our liberty?

CINNA

Heaven, had it wished Rome's liberty unlost,
Would have defended it by Pompey's hand.
It chose his death to serve most fittingly
As an eternal sign of this great change,[2]
And owed it to the shade of such a man,
To bear Rome's liberty away with him.
This word has long served only to delude.
Greatness prevents her from enjoying it.
Since Rome became the mistress of the world,
Since wealth has multiplied within its walls,
And since, fertile in glorious deeds, it's bred
Proud citizens more powerful than kings,
The great, ensuring power by purchased votes,
Richly their so-called masters subsidize,

1. These gates were opened in time of war and closed in time of peace.
2. The institution of authoritarian rule.

Who, willingly enchained in gilded bonds,
Are ruled by those they think that they control.
They live by intrigue, envious each of each,
Which their ambition turns to blood-stained leagues.
Thus Sulla took to envying Marius;
Caesar my grandfather,[1] Antony you.
Thus, liberty can have no further use
Except to feed a raging civil war,
When, by disorders fatal to the world,
Some want no masters, others want no peers.
My lord, Rome to be saved must be as one
Under a leader whom we all obey.
If you still wish to give it heart, remove
The means to sunder Rome within itself.
Leaving the place he had at last usurped,
Sulla but paved the way for Caesar and
Pompey. For this would not have come to pass
Had he but forged hereditary power.
What else did Caesar's murder do but rouse
Against you Antony and Lepidus,
Who would not have made Romans Rome destroy
Had Caesar left the empire in your hand?[2]
If you lay down this power, you will again
Plunge it into the ills it's scarce forgot,
And, of the little blood that's left to it,
Another war will drain it utterly.
Let love of country, pity touch you; let
Your Rome address you, on my knees, through me.
Consider well the price that you have cost.
Not that Rome thinks you are too dearly bought.
For all its ills, it is too well repaid,
But fear, well founded, terrifies its soul.
If, bent on pleasing Rome and tired of power,
You give it back a boon it cannot keep,

1. Pompey the Great.

2. That is, had he appointed Augustus (or Octavius as he then was) as his heir.

If it must buy another master and
If you do not prefer its weal to yours,
If this disastrous gift makes Rome despair,
I dare not tell you what I dare foresee.
Preserve yourself, leaving a master, Sir,
By whom its happiness will be reborn.
The better to promote the common good,
Name a successor worthy of you, now.

AUGUSTUS

Enough of this; my pity wins the day,
I love my peace of mind, but Rome still more.
Whatever great misfortune may ensue,
I'll will my downfall for the sake of Rome.
My heart in vain yearns for tranquillity.
By your advice, Cinna, I'll stay in power;
But *that* I'll do to make you share in it.
I see your hearts are as an open book
For me, and each in the advice he gives
Has but the State and me in mind.
Your love alone prompts your conflicting views,
And here is your reward. You, Maximus,
I name you governor of Sicily.
Go, rule on my behalf that fertile land;
Remember that you govern it for me,
That I must answer here for all you do.
Cinna, accept Emilia as your wife.
You know she is for me what Julia[1] was,
And, if ill fortune and necessity
Have made me treat her father cruelly,
My treasure lavished on her must, since then,
Have softened her resentment at her loss.
See her at my command and woo her. You
Are not a man to be disdained by her.
She'll be enchanted if you seek her hand.
Farewell. I'll bear the news to Livia. Go.

1. Julia was Augustus' daughter, whom he had exiled for misconduct.

Scene Two

CINNA, MAXIMUS

MAXIMUS

What is your plan after these fine harangues?

CINNA

The one I had, the one I'll always have.

MAXIMUS

A chief of plotters flatters tyranny!

CINNA

A chief of plotters wishes it unscathed!

MAXIMUS

I wish to see Rome free.

CINNA

And it is clear
I wish to see Rome freed *and* take revenge.
Must then Octavius sate his furious rage,
Pillage the altars, sacrifice our lives,
Spread horror broadcast, pile Rome high with dead,
And then be quit for half an hour's remorse!
When heaven arms our hands to punish him,
Craven repentance shields him from attack.
No, his impunity merely invites
Some other knave to follow in his steps.
Avenge our fellow Romans. Let his fate
Appal the next aspirant to the crown.
The people must be rid of tyranny.
If it had punished Sulla, Caesar had
Dared less.

MAXIMUS

But Caesar's murder, which you find
So just, excused Augustus' cruelties.
Wishing to free us, Brutus went astray.
Had he not struck, Augustus had dared less.

CINNA

Cassius' mistake, his panic suicide,
Brought back a fierce tyrannical régime.
But such unfortunate mistakes will cease
When Rome is guided by more balanced chiefs.

MAXIMUS

We are still far from offering the proof
That we'll behave more sensibly than they.
Meanwhile it's hardly wise not to accept
Good fortune sought even at the risk of death.

CINNA

It's much less wise to think that one can cure
Malignant growth unless you cut the root.
The use of gentleness for such a cure
Is pouring poison on an open wound.

MAXIMUS

You wish it bloody, and you make it fail.

CINNA

You wish it painless, and you make it base.

MAXIMUS

There never can be shame in breaking chains.

CINNA

Without brave acts, they're broken cravenly.

MAXIMUS

Never did freedom cease to be desired.
It's always an inestimable boon.

CINNA

It cannot be a boon Rome rates so high,
Given by a hand tired of oppressing it.
Its heart's too noble to delight to be
A tyrant's cast-off who was once his prey.
And all of glory's seasoned partisans
Hate him too deeply to accept his gifts.

MAXIMUS

Emilia, then, is hateful to your eyes.

CINNA

Receiving her from him would torture me.
But, when I've taken full revenge for Rome,
I shall defy him even in Hades. Yes,
When I have merited her by his death,
I plan to link my blood-stained hand with hers,
Marry her on his ashes, and transform
The tyrant's presents to his death's reward.

MAXIMUS

How can you ever hope to please her, friend?
She loves Augustus like a father, and
You're not the man to conquer her by force.

CINNA

Friend, in this palace every wall has ears,
And it may be we speak imprudently
Of secrets in a place unsuitable.
Let us go out. I shall discuss with you
The mildest methods to secure my ends.

ACT THREE

Scene One

Emilia's apartment

MAXIMUS, EUPHORBUS

MAXIMUS

He told me so himself. They are in love;
He loves Emilia and she worships *him*.
He must avenge her to obtain her hand;
This is why he involves us in the plot.

EUPHORBUS

Ah! now I understand the violence
With which he makes Augustus stay in power;
The league will crumble if he[1] abdicates,
And all the plotters will become his[1] friends.

MAXIMUS

They vie in serving Cinna's passion. He,
Feigning to act for Rome, acts for himself.
And I, by evil luck undreamed of, serve
My rival, not, as I imagined, Rome.

EUPHORBUS

You are his rival?

MAXIMUS

Yes, I've been at pains
To hide the fact with tolerable skill;
My ardour wished, before it showed itself,
By some great exploit to deserve her heart.

1. Augustus.

He wrests her from me now by my own hands;
I execute his plan which spells my end,
By helping action which will bring me death.
To murder me I offer him my arm;
Into what troubles friendship plunges me!

EUPHORBUS

Escape them, Sir. Take action on your own;
Forestall a fatal plan that ruins you;
Win your belovéd by accusing him.
Thereby you'll save Augustus' life, and then
He cannot well grudge you Emilia's hand.

MAXIMUS

I'll not betray a friend.

EUPHORBUS

All's fair in love;
A lover bent on conquest knows no friends;
Besides, a traitor's there to be betrayed
Who dares betray master for mistress.[1] Come,
He forgets favours. You forget your friend.

MAXIMUS

A crime's example is to be eschewed.

EUPHORBUS

So foul a plan makes all legitimate.
It is not criminal to punish crime.

MAXIMUS

A crime by which Rome wins its liberty!

EUPHORBUS

Fear all things of a mind so cowardly.
The country's weal is not what touches him;
He's fired by selfish interest, not by fame.

1. In the seventeenth-century sense of beloved.

He would love Caesar were he not in love;
In short, he's ingrate, not idealist.
Think you you've scanned the bottom of his soul?
He masked his passion as the public weal,
And may still use that passion to conceal
The odious face of his ambitiousness.
Perhaps he means, after Octavius'[1] death,
To make Rome slave instead of freeing it,
Counting you as his subject even now,
Or on your downfall bases all his plans.

MAXIMUS

But how accuse him and not name the rest?
This revelation would destroy them all,
And thus, most infamously, we'd betray
Those who like us are moved by love of Rome.
I cannot bring myself to do this deed.
Too many guiltless men would pay for him.
I dare to ruin *him*, but fear for *them*.

EUPHORBUS

Augustus, wearied of severity,
Loathes bloody executions. Punishing
The leaders, he will spare the lesser men.
If all the same you fear his wrath for them,
Speaking to him, speak in the name of all.

MAXIMUS

We argue to no point. It's mad to hope
By Cinna's doom to win Emilia's hand,
You will make certain of displeasing her
By sending to his death the man she loves.
I doubt if Caesar will accord me her.
It's not her person but her heart I want,
And do not rate possessing her so high
If I've not conquered her affection. How
Can I deserve her by a threefold crime?

1. Augustus was known as Octavius before he became Emperor.

I'm false to her beloved, baulk her revenge,
I save the life she wishes to destroy;
How could I hope that she would cherish me?

EUPHORBUS

Frankly, that seems to me most difficult.
However, guile may serve your turn in this;
It must be such as to deceive her, though,
And, for the rest, time will suggest a way.

MAXIMUS

But, if he names his fair accomplice[1] and
Caesar should punish her along with him,
Can I, as my delation's price, demand
The hand of her[1] who makes us plot his[2] death?

EUPHORBUS

So many obstacles could be adduced
That to surmount them would need miracles;
And yet I hope that, if we set our minds . . .

MAXIMUS

Go. Here is Cinna. I will join you soon.
I'll make him tell me some particulars,
The better to achieve my purposes.

Scene Two

CINNA, MAXIMUS

MAXIMUS

You seem concerned.

CINNA

I am – not without ground.

1. Emilia. 2. Augustus.

MAXIMUS

May I know why you're so preoccupied?

CINNA

Both Caesar and Emilia rack my thoughts.
One seems to me too cruel, one too kind.
Would heaven that Caesar steered a better course,
Inspired more love in her or loved me less,
That all his kindnesses could touch her heart
And win her over as she conquers me!
I feel my heart transfixed by keen remorse
Which conjures up his countless benefits.
His favour so complete, so ill repaid,
Kills me by unrelenting, fierce reproach.
I see him, worst of all, unceasingly,
Place in our hands his power absolute,
Listen to us, applaud me, say to me:
'Cinna, by your advice, I'll keep my power,
But this I'll do to make you share in it.'
And I would plunge a dagger in his breast!
Ah! rather . . . but alas I worship her.
I'm bound to her by an accursed oath.
Because she loathes him, I must hate him too.
I sin against my honour and the Gods.
I'll be forsworn or kill my patron, and,
Whate'er I do, be false to one of them.

MAXIMUS

A moment past, you were not so distraught;
You seemed resolved in what you planned to do.
You did not feel reproach *then*, or remorse.

CINNA

We feel them when the blow is to be struck;
We do not see the horror of the crime
Until the hand is poised to execute.
Till then the soul, possessed by its designs,
Cleaves blindly to its first idea. But
After the deed, what mind is not appalled?

Or rather who's not overwhelmed by it?
Brutus himself, however much esteemed,
Tried more than once to interrupt his plans.
Before he struck, some tremor of remorse
And of repentance oft assailed his soul.

MAXIMUS

His will was such, he did not feel unease.
He did not tax his hand with thanklessness,
Against a tyrant all the more inflamed,
The more the tyrant loved and favoured him.
You follow in his footsteps. Act like him.
Let your remorse more fittingly denounce
Your craven counsels which alone have checked
The glad revival of our liberty.
You, you alone robbed us of that today;[1]
Brutus would have accepted Caesar's move,
And never let a frivolous concern
Of love or vengeance jeopardize success.
Ignore the voice of him who smiles on you
And wishes you to share his tyrant's power.
But hear the voice of Rome cry at your side;
'Cinna, give back what you've deprived us of;
And if, just now, you put your mistress first,
Do not prefer my tyrant to me.'

CINNA

Friend,
You overwhelm one so ill-starred as I
Who cravenly pursues a grand design.
I know I've robbed my fellow citizens.
I'll soon restore what I have snatched from them.
Forgive an old but dying friendship, for
As it expires, I cannot but be moved,
While waiting for Emilia, if I may,
I'll freely voice my bottomless despair.
My wretchedness must grate on you. It needs
Solitude as the balm for all its ills.

1. By his rejection of Augustus' offer, Cinna has deprived Rome of the chance to recover its republican liberty. See also line 854.

MAXIMUS

You wish to picture now to your beloved
Octavius' kindness and your weakness. Since
Lovers need total secrecy, farewell.
As a discreet confidant, I withdraw.

Scene Three

CINNA

A worthier name give to the glorious sway
Of honour and nobility of soul,
Which puts a bar to over-hasty acts
By my ingratitude and cowardice;
Nay, rather call it[1] weakness as before
Since my beloved makes it become so weak,
That it respects a love it ought to crush,
Or, fighting, dare not triumph over it.[2]
In this extreme, what must I then resolve?
Which way should I incline and take which side?
How hard it is for noble souls to fall!
Whatever fruit I hope to pluck thereby –
The sweets of love, the pleasures of revenge,
The glory gained setting my birthplace free –
Are not enough to make my reason yield,
If they must be acquired by treachery,
If I must murder a great-hearted prince
Who so esteems my lowly character,
Who heaps on me honours and benefits,
And who still reigns on my advice alone.
Unworthy treason! daring enterprise!
May Roman slavery forever last!
Perish my passion; perish, too, my hope,
Rather than such a crime should stain my hand!
Does not he offer everything I wish,
And which my love would purchase with his blood?

1. The sway of honour. 2. Cinna's love.

Must he be murdered for me to enjoy
His gifts? Must I extract what's freely given?
But I am bound by an imprudent oath.
Emilia! Ah! your hate and your revenge –
My troth, my heart, my arm, all's pledged to that.
I can do nothing now but by your leave.
Emilia, *you* must help me steer my course;
You must accord Augustus his reprieve;
Your wish alone decides his destiny,
And in my hands you hold his life and death.
O gods, who make men worship her like you,
Make her, like me, accessible to prayer;
And, since I cannot free myself from her,
Let me incline her to what I desire.
But see, this sweet but heartless one returns.

Scene Four

EMILIA, CINNA, FULVIA

EMILIA

The gods be thanked, Cinna, my fear was vain.
None of your friends has broken faith with you;
I did not have to intervene for you.
Caesar told Livia, in my presence, all,
And by this news he brought me back to life.

CINNA

Will you disown him, and will you delay
Giving effect to his most happy gift?[1]

EMILIA

That's in your hands.

CINNA

Nay, rather, it's in yours.

1. That is, accepting marriage to Cinna.

EMILIA

I'm still myself. My heart has never changed.
Who gives me to you, Cinna, gives you nought;
It merely makes a present of what's yours.

CINNA

You still can wish . . . O heaven, I dare not speak!

EMILIA

What can I wish? What do you fear?

CINNA

I sigh
And tremble. If we wished the same at heart,
I would not need to tell you why I sigh.
Thus I am sure I would incur your wrath;
I dare not speak, but can't be silent.

EMILIA

Speak.
You put me on the rack.

CINNA

I shall obey.
But I shall bring your hate upon my head.
I love you. May the thunderbolt descend
If to adore you is not all my joy
And if my passion burns not with the fire
That such a beauty lights in noble hearts.
But ah! at what a price you give your soul!
My happiness is bought by infamy;
Augustus grants . . .

EMILIA

Enough. I understand.
I see that you're inconstant and repent.
A tyrant's bribes efface your promises.
Your love, your oaths, yield to his bounties, and

You dare to think, in your credulity,
Augustus can do all, can even give *me*.
You want me from his hand, and not from mine;
Think not that thus I ever shall be yours.
He may make the earth tremble 'neath his feet,
Unthrone a king and give his[1] land away,
By his proscriptions redden land and sea,
And at his whim fashion the world anew;
But still my heart is not within his power.

CINNA

That's why I want to owe it but to you.
I'm still myself. My troth is still unstained;
Though feeling pity, I am not forsworn.
I unreservedly obey your will,
And serve your interests more than I have pledged.
I could have, without perjury or crime,
Let your illustrious victim go unscathed.
Caesar, stripping himself of power supreme,
Deprived us of the grounds for killing him.
The plot would have dissolved into thin air,
Your plans miscarried and your hate been foiled.
I alone rallied his astounded soul;
I crowned him as a sacrifice for you.[2]

EMILIA

A sacrifice to *me*, wretch, and you wish
That I restrain your hand and love him too.
I'll be the loot of one who spares his life,
And the reward for forcing him to reign.

CINNA

Condemn me not when I have served you. Now
You could not, but for me, decide his fate.

1. The king's.

2. In this highly involved plea, Cinna is contending that, had Caesar abdicated, there would no longer have been any case for plotting to murder him, and Emilia's desire for revenge would therefore have been unsatisfied.

CINNA

Despite his benefits, love guides my hand.
He can be killed by me or owe his life
To you. In my obedience to you, still
Let me express my gratitude to him;
I'll try to overcome your anger and
Give you the love for him he has for me.
A soul that takes nobility as guide
Abhors ingratitude and treachery.
It hates the infamy of happiness
Bought at the price of honour.

EMILIA

As for me,
I glory in this ignominy and
Approve perfidiousness towards tyranny;
And, when the course of our oppression's changed,
The most ungrateful are the noblest hearts.

CINNA

You but create virtues to suit your hate.

EMILIA

No, I create virtues worthy of Rome.

CINNA

A truly Roman heart . . .

EMILIA

Dares all to end
The life of one who has enslaved it,[1] and
Flees more than death the shame of slavery.

CINNA

To be Octavius' slave's an honour. We
Have often seen kings bowing at our knees
And begging for support from slaves like us.
He humbles at our feet their diadems;

1. Rome.

He makes us sovereign o'er their royalty,
Taking from them tributes to heap on us,
And lays a yoke on them from which we're freed.

EMILIA

A fine ambition you have set yourself!
You think you're something, being more than king!
Throughout the world is there a king so vain
As claims to equal any citizen
Of Rome? Think. Antony incurred their hate,
Dishonoured by his passion for a queen;
Attalus, a great king grown old in power,
Who called himself the freedman of our Rome,
Even though the arbiter of Asia,[1]
Would have esteemed his throne less than that rank.
Recall your name; maintain its dignity,
And, taking on a Roman's gravity,
Learn that no Roman under heaven is born
But to rule kings and to live unsubdued.

CINNA

Heaven has at last only too clearly shown
It blasts ingratitude, hates murderers.
Whatever we may plan or execute,
It sets up thrones but will avenge their fall.
Heaven sides with those whom it has called to power.
The blow that strikes them down takes long to heal;
And, when heaven is resolved, the murderers
Are punished by the thunderbolt alone.

EMILIA

Say you are going over to their side,
Leaving the tyrants to the thunderbolt.
I'll speak to you no more of this. Go, serve
Your tyrant. Sate your craven impulses.
To set your wavering mind at rest, forget
Your birth; forget the prize awaiting you.[2]

1. Asia Minor. 2. Emilia herself.

I'll do without your hand to serve my cause,
And yet avenge country and father. Know
I would have died by now a glorious death,
If love had not so far held back my arm.
It's love that, keeping still its hold on me,
Made me on your behalf preserve my life.
Alone against a tyrant, killing him,
I should have died dismembered by his guards.
I would by death have robbed you of myself;
And, since for you alone love made me live,
I sought in vain to keep myself for you,
And thus enable you to merit me.
Forgive me, though, great gods, if I was strong,
Thinking to cherish Pompey's grandson, and,
By false appearances my mind misled,
I chose a changeling slave instead of him.
But I still love you whatsoe'er you be,
And, if to win me you must now betray
Caesar, thousands would vie in doing so,
If they at the same price could win my hand.
But have no fear I can be conquered so.
Live for your tyrant while I perish yours.
My life, like his, is rushing to its end,
Since your base heart does not dare merit me.
Come, see me bathed in *his* blood and in *mine*,
Escorted only by my fortitude,
And tell you as I die with mind content:
'You are alone responsible, not fate;
Sentenced by you, I to the tomb descend
In glory which was destined to be yours.
Dying, I shall destroy absolutism,
But, had you wished, I would have lived for you.'

CINNA

Well! be it so. You must be satisfied;
Rome must be freed, a father's death avenged;
We must upon a tyrant rain our blows;
But Caesar is less tyrannous than you;

He wrests from us our fortune, life and wives,
And does not tyrannize over our souls.
But the dominion of your ruthless charms
Does violence even to minds and wills.
You make me prize that which dishonours me;
You make me hate what all my heart adores;
You make me shed that blood for which I ought
To offer mine a hundred thousand times.
You wish it so. My word is pledged; but I
At once will turn my hand against myself
And immolate myself to Caesar's shades,
Adding to my forced crime my punishment,
And, by this action, with the other merged,
Retrieve my honour scarce has it been lost.
Farewell.

Scene Five

EMILIA, FULVIA

FULVIA

You've plunged his soul into despair.

EMILIA

Let him stop loving me, or choose aright.

FULVIA

He will obey you if it cost his life.
Lady, you weep.

EMILIA

Alas! run after him
And, if your friendship deigns to succour me,
Extirpate from his heart this plan to die.
Tell him . . .

CINNA

FULVIA

That you will let Augustus live?

EMILIA

Ah! that is asking far too much.

FULVIA

What then?

EMILIA

Let him go on, and do what he has sworn,
And afterwards choose between death and me.

ACT FOUR

Scene One

Augustus' private apartment

AUGUSTUS, EUPHORBUS, POLYCLETES, GUARDS

AUGUSTUS

All that you tell me is incredible.

EUPHORBUS

My lord, even the tale of it appals.
Such raging fury's scarce conceivable,
The very thought brings shudders to the soul.

AUGUSTUS

My dearest friends! What! Cinna, Maximus!
The two I honoured with such high esteem,
To whom I bared my heart and whom I chose
For the most noble, crucial offices!
When I have placed my empire in their hands,
Each one of them conspires to murder me!
Maximus sees his error, has me warned,
And shows by penitence a heart that's touched.
But Cinna!

EUPHORBUS

He alone is adamant,
The more because your bounties weigh on him.
And he alone leads the campaign against
The virtuous remorse of all the rest,
And, though some fear mingles with their regret,
He seeks to win them back to his designs.

AUGUSTUS

He alone works on them, leads them astray!
The falsest man the earth has ever spawned!
O treason in a Fury's breast conceived!
O keenest blow struck by so dear a hand!
Cinna betrays me. Ho! Polycletes.
(He whispers something to Polycletes)

POLYCLETES

Your orders will be carried out, my lord.

AUGUSTUS

And have Erastes summon Maximus
Here to receive my pardon for his crime.
(Polycletes goes in)

EUPHORBUS

He deemed it called for swift self-punishment.
Scarce from the palace had he made return,
Than he began with wild distracted eyes,
His heart swollen with sighs, his breast with sobs,
To curse his life and this detested plot,
Revealing all I have reported. Then
He ordered me to warn you and went out.
'Tell him I'll mete out justice to myself,'
He said. 'I realize what I deserve.'
Then in the Tiber suddenly he plunged.
The rapid swirling waters and the night
Concealed the end of his unhappy tale.

AUGUSTUS

Remorse has weighed too heavy on his soul.
He has himself forestalled our clemency;
All crimes against me penitence redeems.
(To the guards)
But, since he has foregone my pardon, go
And see to all the rest. And take good care
To have this faithful witness guarded well.

Scene Two

AUGUSTUS

Heaven! from now on to whom can I entrust
The secrets of my soul, my life itself?
Take back the power which you conferred on me,
If, giving subjects, it denies me friends,
If it is sovereign rulers' destiny
To see their bounty earn them only hate,
And if your rigour forces them to love
The very men you urge to murder them.
Nothing is sure for kings. They must fear all.
Come to your senses. Pity not yourself.
What! you who have spared naught wish to be spared!
Think of the streams of blood in which you've bathed,
What floods have stained the fields of Macedon,[1]
How much was shed in Antony's defeat,[2]
How much in that of Sextus[3] and recall
Perugia[4] and its people drowned in it;
And summon up, after such butchery,
The blood-stained scenes of your proscription[5] when,
Yourself your kindred's executioner,
In your own guardian's[6] breast you plunged the knife,
And then charge heaven with lack of equity
When you see friends arming to murder you
And when they copy you, plotting your doom,
Outraging rights that you did not respect!
Their treason's just and heaven sanctions it.

1. Refers to the battle of Philippi in 42 BC, when the victorious Antony and Octavius (known later as Augustus) massacred the prisoners captured from Brutus' army.

2. Antony's defeat at Actium in 31 BC in a naval battle.

3. Sextus, Pompey's son, defeated at the battle of Naulochus in Sicily in 35 BC.

4. When Antony's brother took refuge in Perugia, Octavius reduced it by starving it out in 40 BC.

5. Proscription involved death and confiscation of property.

6. C. Toranius, Emilia's father.

Vacate the throne as you acquired it,[1] and
Give back unfaithful blood to faithlessness;
Let ingrates be, having been one yourself.
But how my judgement has deserted me!
What madness, Cinna, pardons *you*, and yet
Accuses *me*? *Your* treason forces me
To keep this power, which is my only crime.
To be chastised – and makes me criminal,[2]
Exalts, to smash it, an ill-gotten throne,
And, covering murder with a shameless zeal,
Bars the State's weal, only to ruin me.
So, I could force myself even to forget![3]
You'd live in peace when you had made me quail.
No, I betray myself to think of it;
Who pardons easily invites offence;
Punish the murder and proscribe the rest.
But what! blood upon blood and death on death!
My cruelty is tired, yet cannot stop;
I wish to terrify and only rile.
Rome's hydra-heads all seek my downfall, and,
If one's lopped off, a hundred others sprout.
The blood of these conspirators when shed
Makes life but more accursed and not more safe.
Wait not till a new Brutus strikes you. Die.
Deprive him of the glory of your fall;
It would be cowardly and vain to live,
If hundreds of brave hearts desire my death,
And, if the cream of Rome's most valiant youth,
Takes it in turn to try and end my days;
Die, for this hate's an ill you cannot cure;
Life's of slight value, and the little left
Is not worth buying at the price of death.
Die, but at least make death spectacular;
Die, you must perish now or slay them all.

1. By murder and violence.

2. By rejecting Augustus' offer to abdicate, Cinna has forced him to go on ruling, which constitutes Augustus' only crime.

3. Cinna's treason.

Put out life's torch in the base ingrate's blood;
And immolate the traitor to yourself;
Contenting his desires, punish his crime;
Make of your death a torment for his soul,
Forced to behold it and enjoy it not.[1]
Rather, let us ourselves enjoy his death,[2]
And, if Rome hates us, triumph o'er its hate.
O Romans! vengeance! power absolute!
O ruthless struggle in a wavering heart,
Which shrinks from everything it ventures on!
Decide the fate of an unhappy prince.
Which path must I then follow, which avoid?
Oh! either let me die or let me reign.

Scene Three

AUGUSTUS, LIVIA

AUGUSTUS

I am betrayed. The hand that murders me
Shatters my steadfastness of mind. Cinna,
Cinna, the traitor ...

LIVIA

Yes, Euphorbus has
Related all. I blenched to hear his tale.
But would you listen to my counsel, though
A woman's?

AUGUSTUS

Ah! what counsel can I take?

1. By seeing Augustus die, Cinna would feel that vengeance had escaped him.
2. In the sense of execution.

LIVIA

Your great severity has borne no fruit,
But has, my lord, made a great stir so far.
No one by others' death has been deterred.
Salvidian[1] killed caused Lepidus[2] to rise.
Next came Murena.[3] Cepion[4] followed him.
The torturing of these two men to death
Did not abate Egnatius's[5] fury. Now
Cinna comes forward and replaces them;
And even the least, the most contemptible,
Have sought nobility in such great plans.
You have in vain punished their insolence.
Try how a pardon works on Cinna, and
Turn his confusion into punishment;
Seek now to follow the most useful course.
His death can anger an excited town:
Mercifulness can heighten your prestige,
And those your rigour would antagonize
Perhaps by your indulgence will be touched.

AUGUSTUS

Let's win them over abdicating power
Which makes us odious, conspired against.
By your advice, I've thought too much on this;
Enough. Never again refer to it.
Rome, sigh no more for your lost liberty;
The chains I forged for you myself I'll break,
And give you back your State more peaceful and
Greater than when I wrested it from you.
If you will hate me, hate me openly;
If you will love me, love me without fear.

1. A lieutenant of Octavius.

2. Lepidus, son of the triumvir of the same name, plotted against Octavius after Actium. It was Salvidian's death which led to the plot.

3. Murena conspired against Augustus in 22 BC.

4. Fannius Cepion also conspired, but was not executed till under Tiberius.

5. Egnatius plotted against Octavius some time after Cepion.

Like Sulla, tired of honour and of power,
I too aspire to end in happiness.

LIVIA

Sulla's example weighs too much with you;
The opposite may well rebound on you;
The untold luck by which he stayed alive
Would not be luck if everyone survived.

AUGUSTUS

Well, if this luck's too great to be my lot,
I'll give my blood to anyone to shed.
After a tempest, one must find a haven;
And I see only two – repose or death.

LIVIA

What! lose the fruit of so much sweat and tears?

AUGUSTUS

What! keep the object of such bitter hate?[1]

LIVIA

My lord, to go to this extremity,
Is more despair than true nobility.

AUGUSTUS

To reign and flatter such a treacherous hand
Is to show weakness more than steadfastness.

LIVIA

It is to reign over yourself; thereby
You show the steadfastness befitting kings.

AUGUSTUS

You promised me a woman's counsel, and
You keep your word, for that indeed it is.

1. The throne.

CINNA

After having destroyed so many foes,
I've reigned for twenty years, and hence I know
What a king's virtues are, each in its place,
His duties, too, in this predicament.
The commonwealth is harmed by such a plot;
The very thought of it is treachery,
A wrong to all his country's provinces,
Which he must then avenge or cease to reign.

LIVIA

Do not give so much ear to passion's voice.

AUGUSTUS

Be less inclined to yield, or aim less high.

LIVIA

Do not reject so firmly sound advice.

AUGUSTUS

Heaven will inspire me as to what to do.
Farewell. We're wasting time.

LIVIA

I'll follow you,
My lord, until my love has won its point.

AUGUSTUS

It's love of greatness makes you so insist.

LIVIA

I love your person, not your fortune. Ah!
(*Augustus goes out*)
He flees me. Let us follow him and prove
That he, by mercy, can enhance his power,
And that, in short, clemency is the mark
Of a real monarch to the universe.

Scene Four

Emilia's apartment

EMILIA, FULVIA

EMILIA

Whence comes this joy? And how unsuitably
My mind despite me is so much at rest!
Caesar has sent for Cinna, yet I feel
My eyes unweeping, undisturbed my heart,
As if an inner voice was prompting me
That everything will be as I desire.
Did I hear, Fulvia, right? Did you say so?

FULVIA

I had convinced him[1] not to end his life,
And, chastened, meek, was bringing him to you,
To make a second onslaught on your wrath.
I was rejoicing when Polycletes,
Augustus' usual aide, came up to him,
Suddenly, softly, without retinue,
And at once to the palace led him off.
Augustus is exceedingly disturbed.
We know not why. Opinions differ, but
It's thought that some great worry preys on him
And that he sends for Cinna for advice.
But what dismays me is, as I have learned,
Two unknown men have seized Evander, and
Euphorbus is arrested, none knows why;
Even of his master rumours go the rounds;
Some say he is a prey to black despair;
Some whisper of the Tiber, then are mute.

EMILIA

How many reasons for despair and fear,
Without my sad heart daring to complain!

1. Cinna.

On each occasion heaven has inspired
The opposite reaction in my heart.
An empty terror filled my heart just now,
And, when I should be trembling, I'm as stone.
I understand. You great and kindly gods
Cannot agree to my dishonour, and,
Forbidding me the slightest sigh or tear,
Sustain my constancy against such blows.
You wish to see me die as valiantly
As when I started this great enterprise;
And I will gladly die as you command,
And in the state of mind you keep me in.
O liberty of Rome! O father's shades!
For my part I've done everything I could.
Against your tyrant I have leagued my friends,
And dared for you more than permissible.
If I have failed, my glory is no less;
I will rejoin you if you're unavenged,
But still so reeking with a noble wrath,
In such a glorious death befitting you,
That it will make you recognize at once
The great heroic race from which I spring.

Scene Five

MAXIMUS, EMILIA, FULVIA

EMILIA

But here is Maximus we thought was dead.

MAXIMUS

Euphorbus misinformed Augustus, and,
Arrested, he admitted everything;
To save me, he pretended I was dead.

EMILIA

And what of Cinna?

MAXIMUS

His most keen regret
Is that Augustus knows your secret plans;
In vain he constantly denies the truth.
Evander has told all to exculpate
His master. Someone comes for your arrest
By Caesar's order.

EMILIA

They are slow to act.
I'm tired of waiting, and will follow him.

MAXIMUS

He's at my house.

EMILIA

Your house?

MAXIMUS

You are surprised.
But learn how heaven is protecting you.
It's an ex-plotter who will flee with us.
Let's seize our chance before we are pursued;
We have a vessel ready on the shore.

EMILIA

Know you me, Maximus, and who I am?

MAXIMUS

As Cinna's friend, I do whate'er I can,
And try to rescue you in this extreme,
You who are all that's dearest to his heart.
Let us escape and save our lives. We can
Later return and wreak revenge for him.

EMILIA

Cinna is one whom we must follow, and
Even to revenge him we must not survive.

Who seeks, after his doom, to save himself
Does not deserve to keep his craven life.

MAXIMUS

What blind despair drives you to these mad views?
O gods! what weakness in so strong a soul!
This noble heart puts up so poor a fight,
But the first setback crushes its resolve!
Recall, recall your heroism sublime;
Open your eyes at last to Maximus –
Another Cinna. Heaven in him gives back
Your lover[1] whom you are about to lose;
And since our[2] friendship makes us but one soul
Love, in this friend, the man that you adore.
With the same ardour he will cherish you
As . . .

EMILIA

You dare love me and you dare not die!
You aim too high, but, whatsoe'er your aims,
At least rise to your aspiration's height.
Cease to flee cravenly a glorious death,
Or to propose to me so base a heart;
Force me to envy perfect constancy;
Make me regret you, since I cannot love.
Display a Roman's utmost vigour, and
Seek to deserve my tears if not my heart.
What! if your friendship comes to Cinna's aid,
Think you it lies in courting his beloved?
Learn, learn from me what friendship's duty is.
Set an example now, or follow mine.

MAXIMUS

Your feelings, too impetuous, explode.

EMILIA

Yours plead too skilfully on your behalf.

1. In the seventeenth-century sense of the person who loves and is loved.

2. i.e. of Maxnimus and Cinna.

You speak even now of a well-timed return
And, though distracted, you can think of love.

MAXIMUS

This love was violent, even at its birth.
It is your lover and my friend I love
In you. And the same fire that burned in him ...

EMILIA

Come, for a clever man, you go too far.
My downfall caused me shock but no dismay.
I am not blinded by my proud despair;
My fortitude is unassailed, unmoved,
And I, unwillingly, see all too clear.

MAXIMUS

What! you suspect me of some treachery?

EMILIA

I do, since thus you force me to reply;
The plan for flight is too complete for me
Not to suspect you of some cravenness.
The gods would rain down miracles on us
If they permitted unencumbered flight.
Flee by yourself, and take your love with you.

MAXIMUS

You say too much.

EMILIA

And I assume much more.
Fear not, though, lest I revel in abuse;
But neither hope to dazzle me with lies.
If, in mistrusting you, I wrong you, come
And die with me to vindicate yourself.

MAXIMUS

Live, fair Emilia, then and let your slave ...

EMILIA

I'll listen to you in the presence of
Octavius. Fulvia, come.
(*Emilia and Fulvia exeunt*)

Scene Six

MAXIMUS

In deep despair,
And meriting an even more harsh rebuff,
What, Maximus, will you resolve? What death
Will conscience choose to punish your deceit?
Illusion must no longer blind you, for,
Emilia dying, everything will out;
Perishing on the scaffold,[1] she alas!
Will crown her glory and your infamy.
Her death will to posterity consign
The memory of your vile faithlessness.
One day has seen you by a pointless ruse
Betray your prince, your friend and your beloved;
And yet the violation of these rights,
Two lovers to a tyrant sacrificed,
Will profit you nothing but shame and rage
Which vain remorse has kindled in your heart.
This is, Euphorbus, all your doing. What
Can one expect from fellows such as you?
A freedman's nothing but a wretched slave;
Changing his status does not change his soul.
Yours is still slavish, and, though freed, did not
Take on a glimmer of nobility.
You forced me to preserve an unjust power,[2]
And to belie the honour of my rank;
My heart resisted, but you worked away
Until your cunning soiled my honesty.

1. An anachronism. There were no scaffolds in Roman times.
2. By causing the plot's failure.

It costs me my renown, my life itself,
And I deserve it for believing you.
But heaven will allow my heart incensed
To sacrifice you to these lovers, and
I am persuaded that, despite my crime,
My blood will be acceptable to them,
If in your own my arm, in righteous wrath,
Wipes out the crime of listening to your pleas.

ACT FIVE

Scene One

Augustus' private apartment

AUGUSTUS, CINNA

AUGUSTUS

Be seated, Cinna, and above all else
Do to the letter what I order you.
Lend me your ear, without disturbing me.
No cry, no word, must interrupt my flow.
Keep your tongue bridled, and, if this constraint
Does violence to your emotions, know
You may at leisure afterwards reply.
On this one point alone content my wish.

CINNA

I shall obey, my lord.

AUGUSTUS

Remember well
To keep your word, and I'll adhere to mine.
Cinna, you live, although your parents were
My father's and my people's enemies.
In their encampment you were born, and when,
After their death, you came into my power,
Their hate, deep-rooted in your youthful breast,
Had made you take up arms against me, and
You were my enemy while still unborn;
You were so still, even when you knew me well.
Your disposition never has belied
The race that put you on the other side.

When possible, you gave full vent to it.[1]
My only vengeance was to spare your life;
I made you prisoner to heap gifts on you.
Your prison was my court, my gifts your chains.
I first restored to you your heritage;
Antony's spoils went to enrich you, and,
As well you know, since then at every turn
For you I've erred in over-lavishness.
Each of the dignities you asked of me
I granted you at once without ado.
I even gave you preference over those
Whose parents were the leaders in my camp
And those who purchased with their blood my throne,
And who had oft preserved my life for me.
In short the treatment I accorded you
Made victors envy vanquished. And, when heaven,
Calling Maecenas home,[2] desired to show
After such boons to me a little hate,
I gave you in this sad mischance his place,
And made you my confidant after him.
Even today when still my wavering soul
Pressed me to abdicate the throne, I took
Advice from Maximus and you alone.
And it was yours I followed against his.
Much more. You had Emilia's hand from me
Today, the finest match in Italy,
And whom my love has raised to such great heights;
Crowning you king, I would have given you less.
This you recall. Such fortune, such renown
Cannot so soon desert your memory.
But Cinna, what one never could conceive,
You still recall it, and would murder me.

CINNA

I, my lord, *I* could be so treacherous?
So cowardly a plan . . .

1. Your disposition. 2. Maecenas died in 8 BC.

AUGUSTUS

Think of your pledge.
Be seated. I have not yet had my say.
If you can, after, justify yourself.
Meantime, give ear and try to keep your word.
You plan to kill me in the Capitol
Tomorrow at the sacrifice, your hand
Giving not incense but a fatal blow.
Half of your men will occupy the door;
The other half lend you support. Is this
Well-based intelligence or poor surmise?
Of all these killers shall I list the names:
Proculus, Glabrion, Virginian,
Pompona, Lenas, Plautus, Rutilus,
Marcellus, Albinus, Icilius[1] and
Maximus, dearest to me after you.
The others are not even worth mentioning –
The dregs of Rome, ruined by debts and crimes,
Constrained by my judicious edicts, who,
Despairing of henceforth eluding them,
If all is not o'erthrown can not survive.
You're silent now, and utter not a word
More from confusion than obedience. Say,
What was your plan? What was your purpose when
You'd felled me in the temple at your feet?
To free your country from the monarchy?
If I interpreted your views aright,
Salvation hangs upon a sovereign who,
Holding all in his hand, all things preserves.
And, if you plotted for Rome's liberty,
You would not have opposed my offer, but
Accepted it on the whole State's behalf,
Not tried to win it[2] as a murderer.
What was your aim then? Reigning in my stead?
That would be a catastrophe untold,

1. An extra line has been inserted in order to list all the ten conspirators named (apart from Cinna and Maximus).

2. Freedom.

If, to ascend the throne and rule the land,
You find in Rome no obstacles but me,
If the State's lot is so deplorable
That you come next to me in eminence,
And if the task of ruling, after me,
Can not fall into better hands than yours.
Turn your eyes inwards. Learn to know yourself.
In Rome you're honoured, loved, and everyone
Trembles before you, wishes you success.
Your fortune's at its height; you can do all;
But even those it irks would pity you
If I abandoned you to your deserts.
Dare to refute me. Tell me what you're worth.
Tell me your qualities, your glorious deeds,
The traits by which I should have been impressed,
And all that raises you above the crowd.
My favour makes your glory and your power.
It alone raises you, alone sustains.
People bow down to *that* and not yourself.
Credit and rank are nil except through me;
To cause your downfall all I have to do
Is to withdraw the hand protecting you.
However, I prefer to yield to you.
Reign if you can, even if it costs my life.
But dare you think that the Servilians,
The Cossas, Paulus and Metellius,
And scores of others, all great hearts who are
The living image of their ancestors,
Will so forget their haughty lineage
As to allow you to reign over them?
Speak. Speak. Now is the time.

CINNA

I'm thunderstruck.
Not that your wrath, or death, can frighten me;
I see I've been betrayed. I ask by whom.
I seek and cannot find the culprit. But
I cannot make that point my main concern.

CINNA

I am a Roman and of Pompey's race.
My father and two sons cravenly slain
By Caesar's death were not revenged enough.
This the one reason for my grand design.
And, since I risk the fiercest punishment,
Expect from me no base repentance now,
Useless regrets or vile unmanly sighs.
Fate smiles on you just as it frowns on me.
I know what I have done, what you must do;
You owe examples to posterity.
You must ensure your safety by my death.

AUGUSTUS

You dare me, Cinna, with high-minded words.
Far from excusing it you vaunt your crime.
Let's see if you are constant to the end.
You know what's due to you, for I know all.
Speak your own sentence. Choose your punishment.

Scene Two

AUGUSTUS, LIVIA, CINNA, EMILIA, FULVIA

LIVIA

You know not yet all the accomplices.
Your dear Emilia, Sir, is one of them.
(*Emilia enters*)

CINNA

It's she herself.

AUGUSTUS

What! you my daughter, too!

EMILIA

Yes, all he did was but to please me. I
Was both the reason and reward for it.

AUGUSTUS

What! does the love I planted in your heart
Already make you wish to die for him?
You leave your sentiments unbounded sway.
You love too soon the man I chose for you.

EMILIA

This love that rouses your resentment, Sir,
Is not the prompt effect of your command,
But flowered without your orders in my heart,
And is a secret over four years old.
Much as I loved him, and he worshipped me,
A stronger hate impelled the two of us.
I never was prepared to give him hopes
Unless he could revenge my father's death.
I made him swear it and he sought out friends.
Heaven dashed the hopes that I had placed in him.
I come to offer you a victim, not
To save his life, saying the crime was mine;
His plotting fully justifies his death.
And all excuse of treason is in vain.
To die with him and meet my father's shade
Is all I hope for, all that brings me here.

AUGUSTUS

Till when and for what reason, O ye gods,
Will you take arms against me from my house?
I drove out Julia for debauchery;
I fondly chose Emilia in her stead.
Like her, she is unworthy of this rank.
One soiled my honour, and one seeks my blood,
And both, taking their passion as their guide,
Were one a strumpet, one a murderess.
Daughter! is this my kindness's reward?

EMILIA

My father had the same reward from you.

AUGUSTUS

Think with what love I reared you as a child.

EMILIA

He brought you up with the same tenderness.
He was your guardian, you his murderer.
It was from *you* I learned the way to crime;
My crime differs from yours in this one point,
Your hand was guided by ambition, while
The righteous wrath with which I was consumed
Was bent on sacrificing you to him.

LIVIA

This is too much. Emilia, stop. Reflect.
He has repaid your father's benefits;
His death whose memory incenses you
Was not the emperor's but Octavius'[1] crime.
Heaven itself absolves us of the deeds
Committed for the crown by crowning us.
And in his sacred rank the past becomes
Just, and the future is legitimate.
Who wins the throne cannot be guilty, and
Whate'er he did or does is sacrosanct.
We owe him all our property, our life,
And never can attack a sovereign.

EMILIA

So in the words I spoke to you just now
I sought to rile, not to defend myself.
Punish, my lord, these crime-inducing charms
Which into ingrates turn your favourites;
Curtail my ill-starred life to make yours safe.
I may lead countless others still astray.
And you will be in greater danger if
I have both love and father to revenge.

1. Octavius was the name used before Augustus became emperor.

CINNA

What! *I've* been led astray by you! Must I
Be now dishonoured by the one I love?
My lord, the truth must out. *I* hatched the plot
Before Emilia ruled over my heart.
She was inflexible to my desires;
To win her then I took another tack.
I stressed her father, your severity;
I offered first my arm, and then my heart.
How sweet is vengeance to a woman's mind.
Thus I attacked, and thus I conquered her.
My lack of merit made her spurn me, but
She could not spurn my arm avenging her.
If she conspired, it was my doing. I,
I am the only author of her crime.

EMILIA

What! Cinna, is it thus you cherish me?
To steal my honour when I have to die?

CINNA

Die, but in dying sully not my name.

EMILIA

If Caesar can believe you, mine is lost.

CINNA

And mine is tarnished if you must lay claim
To all the glory of such noble acts.

EMILIA

Well, take your share of it and leave me mine;
Lessening yours would but diminish it.
Glory and pleasure, torture and disgrace,
All, between fervent lovers, should be shared.
Our souls are two great Roman souls, my lord;
Uniting our desires, we pooled our hate;

CINNA

The keen resentment at our parents' loss
Taught us our duties in the self-same hour;
Our two hearts were as one in this design,
And by our souls together it was forged.
We long together for a glorious death.
You wished to join us. Do not part us now.

AUGUSTUS

Yes, I'll unite you, treacherous ingrate pair,
Worse foes than Antony and Lepidus.
Yes, I'll unite you, since you wish it so.
Your mutual passion must be satisfied;
The world, knowing my purpose, must be stunned
Both by the execution and the crime.

Scene Three

AUGUSTUS, LIVIA, CINNA, MAXIMUS, EMILIA, FULVIA

AUGUSTUS

But finally heaven favours me anew
By saving from the waters Maximus.
Come hither, you, my only faithful friend.

MAXIMUS

Do not, my lord, honour a criminal.

AUGUSTUS

You have repented. Speak no more of crime,
When you have stood between danger and me.
To you I owe the empire and my life.

MAXIMUS

Of all your enemies I am the worst.
If still you reign, my lord, if still you live,

You owe it to my raging jealousy.
Remorse has never even grazed my soul.
To foil my rival, I revealed the plot.
Euphorbus misinformed you I was drowned,
For fear you might have sent for me. I sought
A pretext to mislead Emilia and
To frighten her, and lure her steps abroad.
I thought I would persuade her to elope
By promising revenge for her beloved
Later, but this crude trick misfired,
And merely strengthened her fidelity.
She read my heart aright. You know the rest,
And there's no point in my recounting it.
You see the outcome of my artifice.
But, if my service[1] merits some reward,
Then let Euphorbus die upon the rack,
And let these lovers see me too expire.
Because of him I have betrayed my friend,
Master and mistress, country and repute.
And yet would think my happiness complete
If I can after that[2] punish myself.

AUGUSTUS

My cup is full. O gods, can hostile fate
Still find one of my house to lead astray?
Let it join forces with the powers of hell.
I'm master of myself as of the world;
I am. I wish to be. O days to come,
Preserve for ever my last victory!
I triumph over the most righteous wrath
That ever can be handed down to you.
Cinna, let us be friends. This *I* entreat.
As once, my enemy, I spared your life
In spite of your insane and base design,
I spare you, as my murderer, again.
Let us begin a battle that will show

1. His denunciation of Cinna. 2. Euphorbus' execution.

Which of us best can give and best receive.
You spurn my benefits. I'll double them.
I lavished them on you. You'll drown in them.
Accept Emilia whom I've given you,
And, for the coming year, the consulate.
Daughter, love Cinna thus ennobled, and
Prefer his purple[1] to my purple blood.
By my example, learn to curb your wrath.
A husband should outweigh a father's loss.

EMILIA

I yield, Sir, to this generosity.
Its crystal radiance gives me back my sight.
What appeared justified is now a crime,
And – what death's terror had no power to do –
I feel in me burgeon repentance' flower,
And my heart's prompting gives assent to it.
Heaven has decided your supremacy,
And I, my lord, am the best proof 'tis so.
I dare give this decisive evidence:
Heaven changes me; then it can change the State.
My hate I thought undying ebbs to death;
It's dead. And with a new fidelity
I swear that, from now on, my eagerness
To serve you will replace my enmity.

CINNA

What shall I say when all our trespasses
Instead of punishment receive rewards?
O unexampled clemency that makes
My crime the greater and your power more just.

AUGUSTUS

Cease to prevent us from forgetting it.
The two of you must pardon Maximus.
He has betrayed us all, but still has kept

1. The colour of the edge of the consul's toga.

You innocent[1] and given me back my friends.
(to Maximus)
Resume, beside me, your accustomed place;
Return to favour and to your renown.
Euphorbus must be pardoned by all three,
And let tomorrow marriage crown their love.
If you are jealous, that's your punishment.

MAXIMUS

I'll not complain. That penalty is just.
Your generosity dismays me more
Than your disposal of Emilia.

CINNA

Now
Permit my honour, in my heart reborn,
To vow you loyalty basely forsworn,
For it's so firmly based that, were the skies
To crumble, it would be unshakable.
May the great mover of our destinies[2]
Prolong your days by cutting short our years,
And let me, by an envied privilege,
Lay down my life a hundred times for you.

LIVIA

That is not all, my lord. A flame divine
With a prophetic ray illumines me.
Hear what the gods reveal to you through me.
This is your destiny immutable.
After this action you have naught to fear.
Romans henceforth will gladly bear your yoke,
And the most disaffected will relent
And vie in offering their lives for you.
No base design, no ingrate enviousness,
Will mar the course of your imperial days,
No murderers and no conspirators.
You've found the key that can unlock men's hearts.

1. By revealing the conspiracy.
2. Periphrasis for God.

CINNA

Rome, with a joy profound and visible,
Puts in your hands the empire of the world.
Your royal virtues will convince it that
Its happiness lies in Augustus' rule.
Too long misguided, it's now undeceived,
And longs for nothing but the monarchy.
Temples and altars it prepares for you,
And heaven gives you a place among the gods.
Throughout your empire, all posterity
Will cite you as the noblest of our kings.

AUGUSTUS

I shall accept the augury, and hope
The gods will ever more inspire you so.
Tomorrow let the sacrifices smoke,
Redoubled, under happy auspices.
(*To Cinna and Maximus*)
And let the news reach your conspirators:
Caesar knows all but wishes to forget.

END

THE THEATRICAL ILLUSION

PREFACE

The Theatrical Illusion (1636), though successful in Corneille's own day, was promptly forgotten after his death. He himself, writing at a time when the three unities were becoming a dogma, went so far as to term it 'a strange monster', while Fontenelle, his nephew, wrote it off disdainfully as 'irregular and bizarre'. In the nineteenth century, the stern Guizot dismissed it as not worth a mention, were it not that 'by a remarkable quirk of fate, the date of its first performance entitles us to believe that, at the very moment when he was still so far astray, Corneille was already at work on *The Cid*'.

It was not till the thirties of the present century that some of the dust that had gathered on the play was brushed off. In his admirable *Plaisir à Corneille* (1936), exactly three hundred years after the première, Schlumberger observed that 'for the first and only time in his life, Corneille switched from the playful smile to the uninhibited laugh by developing for all it was worth the traditional comic figure of the boastful Matamore'. Possibly stimulated by Schlumberger's enthusiasm, the Comédie Française staged (in 1937) the unforgettable Jouvet production of the comedy, and the following year Brasillach, in a study which revealed a new and utterly unacademic Corneille, defined the play as incarnating all that was genuine in the seventeenth-century dramatist's 'dreamy and passionate poetry'.

It is not surprising that *The Illusion* had to wait so long for appreciation. It represents, to borrow the title of a chapter from Brasillach's book, 'the triumph of the romanesque' (see the Preface on Corneille), which has until very recently been looked at askance by the French literary establishment. It is only with the advent of the cinema that the romanesque has fought its way back to respectability, or at least acceptability, and, at the same time, accustomed audiences to rapid changes in scene, time and subject.

As it happens, the comedy smacks strongly of the cinema *avant la lettre*. A magician shows a father his missing son's adventures, portrayed on a large shadowy screen by phantoms. These scenes constitute a play within a play, and, just to make matters more complicated, between the events thus evoked and the epilogue (when we are returned to the young man's father), there is another 'screen' performance, this time by the son and his beloved in the dénouement of a tragedy. In other words, there is a second play within a play, and this time it is an illusion two degrees removed from reality, since what we are witnessing is a theatrical performance conjured up on a screen and forming part of an ordinary play.

Needless to say, there is no trace in *The Illusion* of the three unities. The subject, it will be clear by now, is utterly fragmented. The time moves dizzily between past and present. The scene is Shakespearian, and changes repeatedly, but only in conventional terms. Thus, the prison is represented by clapping a pair of handcuffs (or the stocks) on Clindor. The stage-setter has left us the following enchanting description of the scene: 'We need in the centre a decorative palace. On one side, another palace for a magician on the top of a mountain; on the other side of the stage, a park. In the first act a night, a drifting moon, an enchanted mirror, a magician's wand, trumpets, paper cones, a cypress hat for the magician.' The properties, it would seem, of a play like *A Midsummer Night's Dream*.

The main origins of this romanesque setting are clear. The sources are to be found in Spanish literature, and in fact Spanish influence is visible at every step in *The Illusion*. As Professor Mélèse rightly notes, 'the play is completely Spanish in taste'. The central character has a Spanish name – the Matamore (literally, 'the killer of the Moors'), and is dressed in the current Spanish mode, with a huge plume on his hat and an oversized rapier. For, if the *miles gloriosus* can trace his ancestry back to Plautus and beyond, the originals of his many incarnations in France around 1630 all lived on the other side of the Pyrenees.

However, the main interest of the comedy does not lie in its form or origins, but in the youthful vigour and gaiety which course through all the five acts. The verve of the characterization, action and language recalls the inventive exuberance of Rabelais and points forward to the remarkable, if less appreciated, talent of Scarron. Corneille, it is obvious, had not yet been chastened by the opposition to *The Cid* of the 'learned', with their insistence on the rules. Not only does his elation enable him to make of the portrayal of the traditional braggart 'a dazzling success', but he parodies the sabre-rattling of *The Cid* and the bombast of later plays, even before they were written. He uses, says Schlumberger, 'the rhythm, verse and language of *The Cid* to compose the ridiculous threats of the Matamore'. Boileau, when writing a eulogy of Condé, coolly lifted two lines of the Matamore's first long speech:

> My mere name makes the castle's walls collapse,
> Vanquishes squadrons, triumphs on the field.
>
> (lines 233–4)

The other characters do not possess the Matamore's larger-than-life convincingness. But the glib, unscrupulous Clindor is an unusual character, at least for 1636. Despite certain picaresque analogies with other adventurers of the time, he can perhaps be seen more clearly in the perspective of the eighteenth century, with its proteiform Figaro and the enterprising Gil Blas. The pert soubrette, Lyse, too, anticipates (by over a hundred years) Marivaux's delicate, flirtatious bantering.

Lastly, readers' attention should be called to the proud defence of the stage in the final act. Antoine Adam has suggested that Corneille may have been touched to the quick by an attack on the theatre – no unusual event at a time when the Church still regarded the stage as the work of Satan. The warmth of Corneille's apology suggests that he was directly taken to task by some censorious busybody. It is, in any case, fitting that such an unusual and enjoyable work should end on a note of personal commitment.

If there is a French seventeenth-century play which should succeed in making direct contact with the Shakespeare-conditioned Anglo-Saxon public, it is this.

THE THEATRICAL ILLUSION SUMMARY

ACT ONE

PRIDAMANT has had no news for ten years of his son Clindor whom he had driven from home by his harshness, and, in despair, turns to the magician, Alcandre. The magus informs him that the young man is alive, and, having run through the whole gamut of possible occupations, is now acting as go-between for the swashbuckler, Matamore, and his beloved, Isabelle. Alcandre offers to conjure up some of Clindor's adventures, and the proposal is gladly accepted by Pridamant.

ACT TWO

As if on a screen, Alcandre portrays Clindor's amours. Isabelle turns down the advances of a certain Adraste, but pretends to accept those of Matamore. In reality, she has bestowed her affection on Clindor. After a love scene between the two, Adraste appears and insults Clindor who returns a dignified reply. Lyse, Isabelle's maid, is also in love with Clindor. She decides to have him punished out of jealousy. She informs Adraste of Clindor's real identity and of his success in courting Isabelle.

ACT THREE

Géronte, Isabelle's father, orders her to marry Adraste, but she refuses. Matamore overhears a conversation between Isabelle and Clindor and threatens to execute Clindor for his 'treason'. Clindor is not bluffed and soon sends the poltroon about his business. Adraste comes on the scene, supported by his retainers and bent on giving Clindor a beating. Clindor defends himself, runs Adraste through and is arrested and thrown into prison.

ACT FOUR

Clindor is sentenced to death, but Lyse, who has had a change of heart, effects his release by promising to marry the gaoler. After getting rid of Matamore who has remained hidden for four days in Isabelle's house (to make good his escape from the fracas accompanying Clindor's arrest), Isabelle, aided by Lyse appropriates her father's valuables, and the two women flee with their lovers. The evocation of Clindor's first set of adventures by Alcandre ends here.

ACT FIVE

Alcandre now conjures up the same characters but this time in the role of more illustrious personages. Clindor is faithless to his wife. She learns of his infidelity and reproaches him with it. He protests but finally promises to mend his ways. He is set upon by the retainers of the deceived husband, expires, and is followed to the tomb by Isabelle who dies of grief.

At the sight of his son's death, Pridamant is distraught, but he is quickly reassured by Alcandre who explains that the scene is merely the dénouement of a drama and that Clindor and Isabelle are now successful actors. There follows a panegyric of the stage by Alcandre, and Pridamant now expresses his complete satisfaction with his son's career, as well as his undying gratitude to the magician.

DEDICATION TO MADEMOISELLE M.F.D.R.[1]

Mademoiselle,

Here is a strange monster which I am dedicating to you. The first act is only a prologue; the next three constitute an imperfect comedy; the last one is a tragedy. And all of this, sewn together, forms a comedy. Let people dub it a bizarre and extravagant invention as much as they like; it is new; and the grace of novelty often constitutes, amongst our Frenchmen, no small degree of distinction. Its reception did not shame me on the stage, and I dare to say that the performance of this capricious play did not displease you, since you ordered me to address the dedicatory epistle to you when it was printed.[2]

I am in despair at submitting it to you in such a poor state that it is unrecognizable. The amount of mistakes which the printer has added to mine disguises it, or to be more exact, changes it completely. This is the result of my absence from Paris, from which I was recalled on business at the time it was being printed. I was therefore forced to abandon the proofs to the printer's discretion. I beseech you not to read it before you have taken the trouble to correct what you find marked at the end of this epistle. It is not that I have indicated all the mistakes that have crept into the text. There are so many that, if listed, they would have put the reader off. I have confined myself to noting those which could seriously corrupt the meaning and which cannot easily be guessed. As for the others which merely affect the rhyme, the spelling or the punctuation, I felt that the judicious reader would spot them without too much difficulty, and that it was not therefore worth burdening this first page with them. This will teach me not to venture on

1. The identity of the lady is unknown.
2. In 1639.

the printing of a play during my absence. Be kind enough not to disdain this one, however disfigured it may be; and you will oblige me all the more to remain all my life,

Mademoiselle,

The most faithful and passionate of your servants,

CORNEILLE

CAST

ALCANDRE, *a magician*

PRIDAMANT, *Clindor's father*

DORANTE, *a friend of Pridamant*

MATAMORE, *a Gascon soldier, in love with Isabelle*

CLINDOR, *Matamore's follower, and Isabelle's beloved*

ADRASTE, *a gentleman, in love with Isabelle*

GÉRONTE, *Isabelle's father*

ISABELLE, *Géronte's daughter*

LYSE, *Isabelle's maid*

A GAOLER FROM BORDEAUX

A PAGE *to Matamore*

*

CLINDOR, *in the role of* THEAGENES, *an English lord*

ISABELLE, *in the role of* HIPPOLYTA, *wife of Theagenes*

LYSE, *in the role of* CLARINA, *Hippolyta's lady-in-waiting*

ERASTE, *equerry of Florilame*

TROOP OF ADRASTE'S SERVANTS

TROOP OF FLORILAME'S SERVANTS

The scene is in Touraine in the countryside close to the magician's cave

THE THEATRICAL ILLUSION

ACT ONE

Scene One

PRIDAMANT, DORANTE

DORANTE

This wizard who all nature can command
Has chosen as his palace this dark cave.
The night he spreads over these bare, wild haunts
Raises its veil but to an unreal day,
And tolerates, of its uncertain rays,
Only what dealings with the shades will bear.
No further go. His art has placed a bar
Before the rock to all who dare approach.
This gaping mouth's a wall invisible,
Formed of the air, which none can penetrate,
A rampart strong whose fatal frontiers can
Upon a strip of dust lay thousands dead.
More bent on privacy than on revenge,
He strikes all who disturb him or offend;
Despite your eager curiosity,
You must await his leisure to have speech
With him. Each day he stirs abroad. The hour
Is near when he comes forth to take the air.

PRIDAMANT

I'm sceptical, but die to see the man.
I am impatient, but have little hope.
My son, my dearest son for whom I pine,
Whom my harsh treatment forced to part from me,
And whom I've sought for ten years everywhere,
Has hid forever from me where he lives.
Feeling that he was uncontrollable,

I brought my full authority to bear;
I thought he could be curbed by discipline,
And all my strictness did was banish him.
I realized the error of my ways;
Present, I raged, but, absent, mourned his flight;
And soon a father's love made me repent
Fairly of my unfair severity.
I had to seek him far and wide along
The Rhine, Meuse, Seine, the Tagus and the Po.
But my concern for him torments me still,
And all these wanderings were of no avail.
At last, despairing at such labour lost,
Expecting nothing more of human wit,
To set a limit to so many ills,
I've taken counsel of the nether world;
I've seen the leading men in that great art
In which you say Alcandre is so well versed.
They were as highly praised, as he by you;
Not one of them could ease my suffering.
Hell becomes mute when it must answer me,
Or answers nothing, leaving me perplexed.

DORANTE

Do not dismiss Alcandre as commonplace.
His art is such as is possessed by none.
I need not say he bids the thunder peal,
Causes the seas to swell, the earth to quake,
Stirs up the air in myriad swirling clouds,
Against his foes musters battalions, nay,
Makes unknown forces by his magic words
Move mountains and the storm clouds burst in rain,
And two suns shine, each splendid, in the night;
You have no need of such great miracles.
It is enough if he can read your thoughts,
See deep into the future, know things past.
For him there are no secrets in the world;
Our destinies are as an open book.
Myself, like you, I could not credit it,

But scarcely had he seen me he described
My history, and I was stunned to hear
The hiddenmost details of my amours.

PRIDAMANT

You tell me much of him.

DORANTE

And I've seen more.

PRIDAMANT

You seek in vain to raise my spirits, for
My cares and labours fruitlessly will end
With my sad days wrapped in eternal night.

DORANTE

Since I have left my native Brittany
To come and live here as a country squire,
And two years' wooing by a lucky chance
Have won Sylveria and this castle there,
He's never disappointed anyone.
All who consult him, satisfied, depart.
His help is not, believe me, to be spurned.
Besides, he is delighted to oblige
Me, and, I venture to affirm, my prayers
Can make him grant you favours of great price.

PRIDAMANT

Fate cannot suddenly become so kind!

DORANTE

Have better hopes. He's coming out this way.
Look at the wizard; this grave countenance,
Whose lore unequalled nature keeps in thrall,
Has yet from hostile time salvaged no more
Than some gaunt, century-old skin and bone.
Despite his age, his body still is strong,
His movements agile and his bearing straight.

Mysterious forces function in the man
And make each step a miracle of art.

Scene Two

ALCANDRE, PRIDAMANT, DORANTE

DORANTE

Great learnéd spirit, you, whose studious nights
Produce new marvels every day, to whom
Nothing is secret in whate'er we plan,
Who, without seeing us, see all our acts;
If of your art divine the wondrous power
Ever was helpful on my own behalf,
Lighten this grieving father's suffering;
As an old friend, I feel for his distress.
Rennes gave him birth, even as it did to me.
I spent my childhood almost in his arms;
And there his son, of like estate and age,
Was bound to me by close affection and . . .

ALCANDRE

Enough, Dorante, I know what brings you here;
His son is now the cause of all his grief.
Old man, is it not true your absent son
Harrows you by remorse incessantly?
And that your obstinate severity
Banished him from your sight, and tortures you?
In vain repenting of your harshness, you
Everywhere seek your much mistreated son?

PRIDAMANT

Oracle of our age who knows all things,
I cannot hide the causes of my grief;
You know too well my unjust rigour, and
Too clearly read the secrets of my heart.

It's true, I've erred; but, for the wrong I've done,
Such fruitless labours are a heavy price;
Set, in the end, some limit to my pain
And give me back the prop of my old years.
I'll feel he's back if I have news of him;
To go and find him, love will give me wings.
Where is he hiding? Whither should I go?
Even at the world's end, I'd fly to him.

ALCANDRE

Begin to hope; you'll know, thanks to my spells,
What the avenging heavens denied your tears.
You'll see your son again, honoured and loved,
Wresting his fortune from his banishment.
But I'll do more than *tell*. To please Dorante,
I'll even *show* his fortune's eminence.
Greenhorns in magic with their incense and
Outlandish words they claim omnipotent,
Their perfumes, ceremonies and strange herbs,
Slow down our magic action endlessly.
These are but hocus-pocus, after all,
Just to impress you and to frighten you.
I, wand in hand, can do far more than they.
(*He waves his wand, and a curtain is drawn back behind which the finest costumes of the actors are being modelled.*)
Judge of your son by such magnificence.
Well, is a prince more splendidly attired?
And can you still have doubts how great he is?

PRIDAMANT

You pander to a father's tenderness;
Such riches do not tally with his rank,
And his estate could not enable him
To dare to clothe himself so sumptuously.

ALCANDRE

Since brighter stars shine on his fortunes and
As time went by his station has improved,

No one has just occasion for complaint
If he desires to don such clothes as these.

PRIDAMANT

I'll let myself cherish so sweet a hope.
But among these I see a woman's clothes;
Is he then married?

ALCANDRE

I'll relate to you
The story of his hazards and amours.
However, if you feel resolved enough,
As an illusion you could see his life
And all its happenings performed for you
By ghost-like bodies which, infused with life,
Lack neither gesture nor the power of speech.

PRIDAMANT

Do not suspect me of ungrounded fears;
The portrait of the one I seek could not
When I beheld it ever frighten me.

ALCANDRE (*to Dorante*)

Good Sir, forgive me but you must withdraw
And let the story stay between us two.

PRIDAMANT

I have no secrets from so good a friend.

DORANTE (*to Pridamant*)

We must unquestioningly do his will;
I'll wait for you at home.

ALCANDRE (*to Dorante*)

If he sees fit,
He'll tell you all when you two meet tonight.

Scene Three

ALCANDRE, PRIDAMANT

ALCANDRE

Your son was not at once a nobleman;
All his deeds do not do you credit, and
I would be much embarrassed to expose
His plight to any but a father's eyes.
He took some money from you, but this loot
Scarcely sufficed him for a single day;
To pay his way to Paris, he embarked
On selling charms for fever and migraine,
On telling fortunes, too, and thus arrived.
There, on his wits he lived, and does so still.
He started as a letter-writer, then
Rose in the world to be a lawyer's clerk.
Bored by the pen, he dropped it to parade
Performing monkeys at Saint Germain fair.
He took to rhyming. His poetic vein
Enriched the minstrels strung along the Seine.
He then aspired to higher forms of art;
He even ventured into novels, and
Songs for Gautier[1] and gimmicks for Guillaume.[1]
Since then he dealt in dubious medicines and
Trafficked as master-quack in antidotes,
And, back to law, he turned solicitor.
In short, never was Lazarillo of
Tormes[2] so much a master of all trades.
Hardly a fitting story for Dorante!

PRIDAMANT

How kind of you to keep it from his ears!

1. Gautier-Garguille and Gros-Guillaume were both famous actors at the Parisian theatre, the Hôtel de Bourgogne. They died in 1634, a few years before the present play was first performed.

2. The hero of a picaresque Spanish novel (1554).

ALCANDRE

I'll show it not but give you an account
Whose brevity will spare your sense of shame.
Tired of so many fruitless, joyless trades,
Led by his star, he landed in Bordeaux;
There, while he pondered on what craft to choose,
A bravo of the region took him on
To act as go-between in his amours.
This mission set him up in funds again.
He can, by bearing messages, extract
Most skilfully his valiant dupe's doubloons.
Indeed the messenger's turned rival, for
The lady whom he serves has smiled on him.
When I unfold the tale of his amours,
I'll show you him resplendent in his pride
And even in the act he now performs.

PRIDAMANT

My grief is eased already by this hope.

ALCANDRE

He's hid his name during his wanderings,
Changing it to Clindor of Delamont;
It's thus that shortly you will hear him called.
Look on without a word and with no fear.
I tarry though and you're impatient, but
Do not mistrust me now on that account.
An ordinary spell has no great power
Over the speaking ghosts I must evoke.
Let's go into my cave. I must prepare
New spells for such unprecedented ends.

ACT TWO

Scene One

ALCANDRE, PRIDAMANT

ALCANDRE

Whatever meets your gaze, be not afraid.
Above all, do not leave before I do;
If not, you die. But look. Here comes your son
And then his master, as two spectral forms.

PRIDAMANT

O God! My soul's about to fly to him.

ALCANDRE

Be silent, Sir, and listen to him speak.
(*Alcandre and Pridamant withdraw to one of the wings.*)

Scene Two

MATAMORE, CLINDOR

CLINDOR

What, Sir, you dream of fame? This lofty soul
After so many exploits cannot rest?
Are you not tired of slaying warriors?
You need new laurels to adorn your crown?

MATAMORE

It's true. I muse and cannot yet resolve
Which of the two I first should pulverize –
The Mogul or the Shah of Persia?

CLINDOR

Ah! Pity, Sir, allow them to live on.
What would their death add to your great renown?
Besides, when could you muster all your troops?

MATAMORE

My troops? Ah! coward, villain! For their death
Do you believe this arm's not strong enough?
My mere name makes the castle's walls collapse,
Vanquishes squadrons, triumphs on the field.
My heart, unconquered, against emperors
Arms but the half of its least furious rage;
With one sole order given to Destiny,
I rob the states of their most puissant kings;
The thunder is my cannon, and my troops
The Destinies. With one slight blow I slay
An army. I reduce their plans to smoke.
And yet you dare to talk to me of troops!
You shall no longer serve a second Mars;
I'll slay you with a single of my looks,
Base rogue. However, thoughts of my beloved
Soften my heart. My anger now abates,
And Venus' archer who subdues the gods
Has driven off the death lodged in my eyes.
Look. I have dropped this terrible aspect
Which massacres, destroys, blasts, breaks and burns.
And, thinking of the fair whom I adore,
I am dissolved in beauty, grace and love.

CLINDOR

O Gods! You can be everything at once,
As handsome now as you were terrible!
There is no woman, how austere she be,
Who could hold out against you constantly.

MATAMORE

I once again command, be not alarmed.
At will, I terrify; at will, I charm.

According to my humour, I inspire
Men with affright and women with desire.
When my good looks I could not lay aside,
Their persecution drove me to despair;
I could not issue forth but they would swoon;
Thousands died daily of their love for me.
With all princesses I had rendez-vous;
Queens vied in begging for endearments. Those
Of Ethiopia and of Japan
With their hearts' sighs mingled my name alone.
Passion-struck, two sultanas raved for me;
To see me, two fled from the harem. This
Spoiled my relations with the Grand Seigneur.[1]

CLINDOR

His anger only did you credit.

MATAMORE

But
These goings-on disturbed my martial plans,
And might impede me in my conquest of
The world. Besides I tired of them. And so,
I sent off Destiny to tell his Jove
To find a means to end these outbursts and
These ladies' tiresome importunities.
For otherwise my wrath would strike the heavens,
Deprive it of the empire of the gods
And give his thunderbolt to Mars to wield.
The terror I inspired soon made him yield.
What I desired was granted there and then;
Since then, I'm only handsome when I wish.

CLINDOR

The billets-doux I'd carry but for that!

1. The Turkish Sultan.

MATAMORE

Never accept them, whatsoe'er they be,
Except . . . You understand. What does she say?

CLINDOR

You are the charm and terror of all hearts;
If but your promises can be fulfilled,
Her lot is happier than a goddess's.

MATAMORE

Listen. Back in the days I told you of,
Goddesses, too, were subject to my sway;
And I'll relate a strange adventure which
Played havoc with the universe and caused
Such wild confusion as there never was.
The Sun for a whole day could not even rise,
And that bright, visible, much-worshipped God
Could not to guide its path find any Dawn.
They sought it everywhere – in Tython's[1] bed,
In Cephalos'[2] fair woods, in Memnon's[3] hall.
Since that fair harbinger could not be found,
The world till mid-day was deprived of light.

CLINDOR

Wherever could the queen of brightness be?

MATAMORE

Right in my chamber, offering me her charms,
Wasting thereby her time as well as tears.
My heart was steeled against her potent spells;
And all she gained by her light-hearted love
Was a command to bring the daylight back.

1. Son of Laomedon and husband of Aurora, the Dawn.
2. Son of Aurora and Tython and prince of Ethiopia.
3. Son of Mercury and Creusa, who was loved by Aurora.

CLINDOR

Yes, this strange incident comes back to me.
It was in Mexico I learned of it;
They said that Persia, furious at this slight
To its great Sungod, Sir, complained of you.

MATAMORE

I heard as much. I would have punished them
But I was busy in Bulgaria,
Where their ambassadors' apologies
And presents managed to appease my wrath.

CLINDOR

How magnanimity becomes you, Sir!

MATAMORE

But gaze, my friend, upon this visage, gaze;
You'll see in it virtue's epitome.
Of all the foes humbled beneath my feet,
Whose race has perished, vanished from the earth,
There's none but owes his downfall to his pride.
Those who do homage to my perfect rule
Have kept their States by their submission. Thus,
In Europe kings are civilly disposed.
I do not raze their castles or their towns;
I let them reign. But, among Africans,
Whenever I have found a king too vain,
I've laid the country waste to punish him;
And those vast deserts, endless miles of sand
That man can barely cross, are eloquent
Of my just fury's devastating power.

CLINDOR

Let's talk of love. Here your belovéd comes.

MATAMORE

That cursèd rival never leaves her side.

CLINDOR

Whither are you withdrawing?

MATAMORE

He's not brave,
But he has that which makes him insolent.
Perhaps, triumphant at escorting her,
He might be vain enough to challenge me.

CLINDOR

That would be really courting his demise.

MATAMORE

When my good looks are on, my valour goes.

CLINDOR

Cease to be handsome, and be terrible.

MATAMORE

You do not see what's bound to happen then.
I cannot well be terrible by halves;
I'd kill both my belovéd and my foe.
Let's wait here in this corner till they part.

CLINDOR

Your wisdom, like your valour, is most rare.

Scene Three

ADRASTE, ISABELLE

ADRASTE

If that be so, then what ill fate is mine!
I make no headway by my constancy.
Despite my transports of impassioned love,
You still will not believe I worship you.

ISABELLE

I do not know what you reproach me with.
I think you love me and I'm lovable.
Your ardent sighs are more than eloquent;
And, even if I did not have that proof,
If I at all esteem a gentleman,
I show I do and take him at his word.
Then do as you are done by. Since from you
I have hid nothing of my sentiments,
Do me the favour and believe me when
I tell you I do not return your love.

ADRASTE

This, cruel one, is the unjust reward
That you bestow on me for years of love?
My faithful service is so criminal
As to be punished by eternal scorn?

ISABELLE

Often we give a different name to things.
What you term roses are but thorns for me;
What you call service and affection is
For me sheer persecution and the rack.
Each one persists in his belief. You think
A suit that bores me is obliging me;
What you deem worthy of a great reward
For me deserves but hatred and contempt.

ADRASTE

To show but scorn for such a sacred fire –
A passion heaven first inspired in me.
Yes, heaven at the moment of my birth
Gave me a heart but to adore you with.
Your image was imprinted on my soul.
Before I saw you, you possessed me quite,
And, when to such sweet glances I succumbed,
I gave you nought but was entirely yours
And was assigned to you by heaven's command.

ISABELLE

Heaven would have pleased me giving it elsewhere;
It made you to love *me*, me to hate *you*.
We should be careful not to disobey,
For after all you must have earned its hate,
Or it is punishing a secret crime,
For there can be no torture so acute
As loving when one's love is not returned.

ADRASTE

Since you're aware of all my sufferings,
Will you refuse the pity due to me?

ISABELLE

Of course I won't. I pity you the more
Because these torments seem superfluous,
And harvest as their only recompense
The irksome honour of sad constancy.

ADRASTE

Your father backs me, and, if you persist,
I'll have recourse to his authority.

ISABELLE

That's not the way, Sir, to secure your ends;
Such a fine plan would bring you only shame.

ADRASTE

I hope to see before the day is done
What, in despite of love, his will can do.

ISABELLE

I hope to see before the day is out,
A suitor overwhelmed by some new blow.

ADRASTE

What! Will this rigour never have an end?

ISABELLE

Go. Find my father but leave *me* in peace.

ADRASTE

Your heart, repenting of past iciness,
Will not relent without some show of force;
I'll go this very moment, but will swear
That what I do is all by your command.

ISABELLE

Be off and carry on your vain pursuit.

Scene Four

MATAMORE, ISABELLE, CLINDOR

MATAMORE

The moment that he saw me, he took flight!
That very instant he made way for me!

ISABELLE

That is no shame for him. Kings do as much,
At least if all the rumours of your deeds
And feats of arms did not deceive my ear.

MATAMORE

You can believe them, and, to testify
How true they are, choose where you wish to reign.
This arm at once will carve you out a realm.
I swear it by that arm. Need I say more?

ISABELLE

O squander not its e'er victorious power;
I wish to reign over your heart alone.
All the ambition that my love inspires
Is to hold sway over your soul's desires.

MATAMORE

Lady, they all are yours. To demonstrate
Over them your complete authority,
I will no longer heed this conqueror's urge,
And, leaving monarchs' crowns upon their heads,
I shall take two or three as menials
Who, on their knees, will hand you billets-doux.

ISABELLE

Such glamour would make others envious
Of the unheard-of bliss in which I lived;
And our discreet affection's interchange
Needs only him to bear these messages.
(*She points to Clindor.*)

MATAMORE

You have, God's wounds, a pretty turn of speech.
You find, like me, that greatness is a bore.
The fairest sceptres have no charms for me;
I give them back as soon as they are won,
And I have seen of princesses by the gross
Spellbound by me without my wanting them.

ISABELLE

On this one point, pardon my disbelief.
You left a host of princesses for me!
And you withheld from them a heart that's mine!

MATAMORE (*pointing to Clindor*)

I think that Delamont can say. Come here.
In China at that famous tournament,
The King's two daughters cast their eye on me.
What did they say to you at court of this
Infatuation of the royal pair?

CLINDOR

Both of them died from your unfeelingness.
I was in Egypt when I heard the news,

And then it was that terror of your arms
Made Cairo swim in oceanic tears.
You had just felled ten giants in a day;
You had laid waste the country round about,
Razed fifteen castles, flattened two high peaks,
Set fire to towns, villages, countrysides,
And laid an army near Damascus low.

MATAMORE

How well you note both time and place, my boy.
I had forgotten it.

ISABELLE

Can such great feats
Expunge themselves thus from your memory?

MATAMORE

Laurels wrested from kings encumber it.
I do not burden it with minor deeds.

Scene Five

MATAMORE, ISABELLE, CLINDOR, PAGE

(*The page enters*)

MATAMORE

What do you want?

PAGE

A courier waits without.

MATAMORE

Whence comes he?

PAGE

From the Queen of Iceland, Sir.

MATAMORE

Ah! how I'm persecuted by the Queen!
Oh for some more repose and less good looks!
Grant that my scorn may disillusion her.

CLINDOR

See what this warrior's turning down for you.

ISABELLE

My doubts are at an end.

CLINDOR

He told you so.

MATAMORE

In vain she begs me. I will not accept.
Whate'er her insane hope may promise her,
I'll send her by a letter to her doom.
Allow it to be so, my queen. Meanwhile,
My dear confidant here will for an hour
Talk to you. As he knows my history,
He'll show you what a conquest you have made.

ISABELLE

Don't be so long. The speed of your return
Will show the measure of your love for me.

Scene Six

CLINDOR, ISABELLE

CLINDOR

Or rather show the fellow's character.
That page is kept just for this pleasantry,
To come from time to time and warn my lord
That there's a courier or ambassador.

ISABELLE

This message pleases me more than he thinks;
The madman gone, we two are left alone.

CLINDOR

This favourable hint emboldens me
To make good use of such a chance to speak.

ISABELLE

To tell me what?

CLINDOR

I worship Isabelle,
I have no heart, no soul, but it is hers;
My life . . .

ISABELLE

There's no need to go on. I know,
And I believe these vows. What would you more?
I spurn for you a royal diadem,
Disdain a rival; in a word, I'm yours.
Uncertain passions in their earliest days
Need to protest undying fervour, but
All that our love demands is that we meet.
Your glance says more than all the others' talk.

CLINDOR

Gods! Who would e'er have thought my cruel fate
Would smile so kindly on my loving heart!
Driven by my father's rigour from my home,
Without support or friends, in poverty,
Reduced to pandering to the caprice
And arrogance of such a histrion as
My master is, my pitiable plight
Does not displease or trouble you. Nor can
A well established rival's rank and wealth
Obtain from you more than my ardour does.

ISABELLE

It's thus that one must choose. Real passion clings
Only to what appears worth loving, and
The man who covets rank or property
Loves only for ambition or for greed,
And sullies by this base adultery
The noblest aspirations of great souls.
I know my father takes a different view
And will oppose our search for happiness,
But love is lodged too firmly in my heart
For me to listen to my family.
My father can do much; I can do more.
He chooses for himself. I choose for *me*.

CLINDOR

Embarrassed at your kindness to my poor . . .

ISABELLE

Here comes my pesterer. Let me escape.

Scene Seven

ADRASTE, CLINDOR

ADRASTE

How lucky you and how unlucky I!
Isabelle bears with you, but flees from me.
Whate'er her pleasure in your company,
As soon as I appear, she vanishes.

CLINDOR

She did not notice you approaching, but,
Weary of my remarks, took leave of me.

ADRASTE

Weary of your remarks! You are too nice

And much too witty to bore anyone.
What did you say that could importune her?

CLINDOR

What you can very easily divine.
My lord's amours, or nonsense I should say,
His dreamed-up conquests and his lofty deeds.

ADRASTE

Would you oblige me? Neither he nor you
Are really such as to cause jealousy.
But if you cannot stop his antics, try
To steer his lunacy to other haunts.

CLINDOR

What! Do you fear a man whose compliments
Speak but of death and pillaging, in which
He smites, lays low, breaks, beats, strangles and burns.

ADRASTE

Despite your job, you seem a decent man.
You would not serve, just for the fun of it,
A braggart madder than his idle talk.
How'eer that be, since you've been seeing her,
She treats me more and more unfeelingly.
Either you serve some other, or your rank
Does not accord with your too daring plans.
I much suspect you of deep craftiness.
Your master, to conclude, must woo elsewhere,
Or, if he cannot bring himself to change,
Let him employ some other go-between.
It's not that, after all, this whole affair
Cannot be settled by a father's will;
But of this one small worry ease my mind,
And, if you love yourself, begone from here.
For, if I see you at that door again,
This arm can deal with people of your sort.

CLINDOR

Do you imagine *I* can cut you out?

ADRASTE

Don't answer back, or else the sparks will fly.
Be off. That's clear?

CLINDOR

Well, for a slight offence,
This is no way to treat a valiant heart.
Heaven may not have given me noble birth,
But honour and a spirit resolute.
And, some fine day, I'll settle all my debts.

ADRASTE

You threaten me?

CLINDOR

No, no. I will withdraw.
This cruel slight will not avail you much,
But this is not the place for a dispute.

Scene Eight

ADRASTE, LYSE

ADRASTE

This rascal, Lyse, is still defying me.

LYSE

If you believe *that*, Sir, your mind is sick.

ADRASTE

What! sick, my mind?

LYSE

Yes, sick. It's jealous of
This prince of madmen's wretched serving-man.

ADRASTE

I know my worth and that of Isabelle;
I have no fears of being ousted by
A serving-man. But I won't tolerate
The pleasure she derives from seeing him.

LYSE

You want to have the best, Sir, of both worlds.

ADRASTE

Call, if you will, my sally indiscreet;
Think my suspicions justified or not.
I've driven him out to gain my peace of mind.
But, really, what's the truth?

LYSE

If I dare speak,
Isabelle is in love with him alone.

ADRASTE

What, Lyse!

LYSE

He is the master of her heart.
Never was budding passion more intense.
They're dying to be in each other's arms.

ADRASTE

Ungrateful woman, base, insensate, false;
You chose, then, to prefer a rogue to me?

LYSE

This rival's even more high and mighty. And,
If I may be completely frank with you,
He says he's a rich nobleman.

ADRASTE

The cheek!

LYSE

Fleeing a father's harsh authority,
He has for long been on the go, but now
At last, from lack of funds or from caprice,
He's been engaged by our bold Matamore.
Feigning to further these insane amours,
He has intrigued so cunningly and has
Enchanted so this poor misguided soul,
That all your ardour's zeal has gone for nought.
Speak to her father, though, and soon his power
Will bring her back to duty's bounds.

ADRASTE

I have
This very moment been assured by him
That I shall reap the fruits of constancy,
And, before long, will see the outcome. But,
Listen, you must oblige me even more.

LYSE

If I can help, I will dare anything.

ADRASTE

Arrange to have them caught while making love.

LYSE

Nothing more easy. Even perhaps tonight.

ADRASTE

Goodbye. Remember I must see them both.
(*He gives her a diamond.*)
Meanwhile accept this as a small advance.

LYSE

And let this gallant be most soundly thrashed.

ADRASTE

Believe me, he will be, for your content,
Laden with as much wood as he can bear.

Scene Nine

LYSE

He thinks he's home, the arrogant young fop,
But he will rue he ever turned me down.
Because he's handsome he's a little god.
He only courts young ladies of nobly born.
I don't deserve the honour of his heart;
Nothing will do for him but mistresses[1].
I'm but a maid, and what's he but a groom?
His looks are good, but mine are not that bad.
He says he's rich and noble. What a laugh!
For anyone can say so, far from home.
Even if he is, this evening we may see
His rank and wealth dance to the baton's tune.

Scene Ten

ALCANDRE, PRIDAMANT

ALCANDRE

Your heart beats somewhat?

1. Mistresses is used here in opposition to maids.

PRIDAMANT

Yes, this fearful threat . .

ALCANDRE

Lyse loves Clindor too much to do him ill.

PRIDAMANT

She's spurned by him and seeks to take revenge.

ALCANDRE

Fear nought, for love will make her change her plans.

ACT THREE

Scene One

GÉRONTE, ISABELLE

GÉRONTE

Restrain your sighs and dry your tears, my child;
These are but feeble arms against my will.
My heart, much as it feels for all your woes,
Listens to reason and ignores your tears.
I know better than you what's good for you.
You scorn Adraste since he appeals to me,
And, since I think that you should marry him,
Your pride sees nought in him worthy of you.
What! is he lacking riches, valour, rank?
Is it his face or mind you do not like?
He does you too much honour.

ISABELLE

Yes, I know
He's perfect; and I should feel honoured, but,
If you would kindly let me state my case,
Just a few words to justify myself,
By a deep instinct I can not define,
I should esteem but feel no love for him.
Often this certain something heaven inspires
Stirs up our heart against what is desired
And does not leave us able to obey,
When someone's chosen for us it makes us hate.
It binds together by affinities
On earth the souls that had been matched in heaven.
No union should be made without its seal,
And there's no bond where this approval lacks.

To flout the rulings of this providence
Is to cast doubt upon its wisdom and
To rise against it, to invite its wrath
And all the ills that follow in its wake.

GÉRONTE

Insolent girl, so this is your defence!
What master taught you this philosophy?
You know a lot, but all your knowledge, child,
Will not induce me not to use my power.
If heaven for my choice inspires such hate,
Has it for this great captain fired your heart?
Does this bold warrior hold you in his thrall?
Has he subdued the universe for you,
This braggart who'll ennoble me and mine?

ISABELLE

I beg you, do not treat your daughter so!

GÉRONTE

What urges you to disobey my word?

ISABELLE

Father, my happiness, my peace of mind.
What for you is a happy marriage is
For me a hell to which I am condemned.

GÉRONTE

How many prettier girls there are than you
Who'd gladly be in such a pleasant hell.
In any case, I wish it. You'll obey.

ISABELLE

Put my obedience to a different test.

GÉRONTE

Don't answer back. For I shall have it so.
Go in. We've had enough of argument.

Scene Two

GÉRONTE

What curious fancies youth has nowadays!
It feels its duty as a tyranny,
And the most sacred rights are powerless
To curb this pride which binds it to its course.
The female's nature is to contradict,
Stubbornly rejecting our authority,
Follow only her whim in sentiment,
And never show approval of our choice.
Do not, however, hope, unthinking, blind,
To see me yield to your rebelliousness.
(*Sees Matamore approaching.*)
But will this madman still importune us?
By force or guile I must get rid of him!

Scene Three

GÉRONTE, MATAMORE, CLINDOR

MATAMORE

Am not I to be pitied for my lot?
I'm still pursued by the Grand Vizier;
Tartary, too, summons me to her aid,
Calicut every day appeals to me;
To help them all, I'd need to be four-armed.

CLINDOR

Then leave them to their own devices, Sir,
For you would waste your blows invincible
If, to serve one, you made three jealous kings.

MATAMORE

You're right. Enough of such considerateness!
Only in love should I cause jealousy.
(*He suddenly catches sight of Géronte.*)
Ah! pardon, Sir, if, overlooking you
Although so near, I did not bow to you.
But what distress is painted on your cheek?
Where are your foes? I'll make mincemeat of them.

GÉRONTE

Thanks be to God, I have no enemies.

MATAMORE

Thanks to my arm, which has subdued them all.

GÉRONTE

That favour, Sir, I did not know about.

MATAMORE

Since I've come down so firmly on your side,
They all are dead of fear, or dare not stir.

GÉRONTE

You should be gathering laurels somewhere else.
This arm more dreaded than the thunder is,
I see, inactive in these times of war,
And it's no way to make a glorious name
To stay and loaf about behind the lines.
Everyone thinks your glory is usurped,
And they regard you as a swaggerer.

MATAMORE

Zounds! that is true, and you're entirely right.
But how can I who am in prison leave?
Isabelle holds me here, and her bright eyes
Have made my heart, vanquished, hang up its arms.

GÉRONTE

If nobody but she detains you here,
You're free to start your packing undisturbed.
She's not for you. Don't worry about her.

MATAMORE

Zounds! what is this? I want to make her queen!

GÉRONTE

I'm in no mood to laugh and laugh again
At the grotesque account of your exploits.
Nonsense is pleasing only when it's new.
Make someone else than Isabelle your queen.
If I should catch you courting her again . . .

MATAMORE

He's lost his senses, talking to me thus.
Poor man. Do you not know my dread renown
Makes the Great Turk turn tail, the Devil quake,
That in a moment I can wipe you out.

GÉRONTE

Here is my house. My servants are on call,
Who, since they have no mind to bandy words,
Would answer empty boasts with solid blows.

MATAMORE (*to Clindor*)

Tell him my prowesses on countless fields.

GÉRONTE

Goodbye. Sing small. You'll feel much better then.
Although I am no enemy of yours,
I'm quick to act, my servants to obey.

Scene Four

MATAMORE, CLINDOR

MATAMORE

Respect for my belovéd stays my hand;
To what a pretty pass I am reduced.
Why have I not more rivals (rather than
A father) whom without offending her
I could undo. Skinny old spectre, fiend,
You imp of Satan, image of the damned!
You dare to banish me, and with what threats,
Me, when all kings petition me for help.

CLINDOR

While he is gone, go in without delay;
Talk to your love, have the last laugh on him.

MATAMORE

God's blood! His servants would be insolent.

CLINDOR

Your sword would quickly bring them all to heel.

MATAMORE

Yes, but the flames it casts when it is drawn
Would in a moment set the house on fire,
Devour at once the gutters and the slates,
Ridges and battens, rafters, soffits, stiles,
Crosspieces, lintels, columns, hoists, and jambs,
Purlins, supports and girders, sills and beams,
Doors, railings, bolts and locks, and tiles and stones,
Lead, iron, plaster, paint, marble and glass,
Cellars, walls, courtyards, steps, halls, garrets, rooms,
Pantries and closets, terraces and stairs.
Just think how my enchantress would react;

These fires would quench her ardour and her love.
Go speak to her, you who are valorous;
You risk much less, chastising insolence.

CLINDOR

That would . . .

MATAMORE

Goodbye. They're opening a door
I fear the rabble lacks respect for me.

Scene Five

CLINDOR, LYSE

CLINDOR (*alone*)

This sovereign poltroon to frighten whom
A leaf, a shade, a vapour will suffice,
An old man can insult him, and a girl
Can make him flee. He's scared of being thrashed.
(*He sees Lyse.*)
How dangerous, Lyse, your approach must be.
It strikes a chill into that valiant heart,
That nonpareil, that flower of soldiery,
Who conquers kings as he entrances queens!

LYSE

My face has hardly brought me fortune. Mine
Chills near at hand. Others charm from afar.

CLINDOR

It frightens madmen, but it charms the wise.
There are not many faces such as yours.
If you make conquests, there's good reason why;
I never knew a more attractive girl,
Witty, nimble, adroit, a sense of fun,

A splendid figure (not too plump, too thin),
A good complexion, features delicate,
Entrancing eyes, who would not fall for you?

LYSE

Since when have I become so beautiful?
Take a good look. I'm Lyse, not Isabelle.

CLINDOR

The two of you share all my store of love.
I worship both *your* beauty and *her* wealth.

LYSE

You ask too much. One must suffice for you.
Her wealth takes precedence over my charms.

CLINDOR

Whatever my desire to marry her,
Think you I really love her more than you?
Marriage and love differ as chalk from cheese.
One seeks delight, and *one* convenience. I
Am badly off, and you're not well-to-do.
Two zeroes don't add up to more than nil.
In spite of all the bliss that love distills,
Poor lovers' pleasure never lasted long.
Hence, to succeed, I seek another's hand.
But, if I look at you, I feel a twinge,
And a deep sigh despite me rends my heart,
Which says my reason stifles its desires.
Your slightest glances leave me quite enthralled.
Ah! how I'd love you, if to love were all,
And how you'd please me, if to please were all!

LYSE

How wise you'd be, if you could hold your tongue,
Or till some other time at least put off
Showing with so much reason so much love!
How grand for me to have a suitor who

From sheer compassion does not court me, and
Bears his addresses to a better match
For fear we jointly sink in poverty.
Such striking merits I will ne'er forget.
Continue, meanwhile, with your round of calls.

CLINDOR

How pleasanter a life would be with you!

LYSE

My mistress is alone, and waits for you.

CLINDOR

You drive me out!

LYSE

No, but I send you to
A place where you'll have longer happiness.

CLINDOR

You're so attractive even in disdain.

LYSE

Ah! how you squander so much precious time.
Be off!

CLINDOR

But, if I love another, that's ...

LYSE

For fear of adding my poor lot to yours.
I've told you once that I shall not forget.

CLINDOR

Goodbye. Your banter is so exquisite
That more and more my heart's enslaved to you,
And, if I stayed, your love would conquer all.

Scene Six

LYSE

The ingrate. Finally he looks at me;
He feigns to love me to amuse himself.
After ignoring me, he pays me court,
But in a mood of sheer flirtatiousness,
And, openly admitting he's untrue,
Swears he adores, but will have none of me.
Woo right and left, villain, and share your heart.
Choose whom you want to marry or to court,
And let your interest govern your desires,
But don't think either of us is deceived.
She deserves better than a scheming heart,
And I better than one who loves for gold.
I answered joke with joke, but only so
That my resentment would be hid from you.
A scene would merely cause suspicion. He
Who masks his anger makes his vengeance sure.
And my feigned sweetness is to bait the trap
Into which, very soon, I'll see you fall.
And yet what have you done I should condemn?
To seek one's fortune, is it then a crime?
You love me, but you cherish riches more.
These days, who would not do the same as you?
Forget this scorn he drives himself to feel.
Let him enjoy the happiness that he
Deserves. Love and disdain divide his soul,
And I must spare him if I love him still.
How mad concern for him leads me astray!
Why should I pardon such ingratitude?
O! thirst for vengeance. How can you relent,
And let my anger, that should triumph, flag?
He loves me, yet he brushes me aside.
I love him, and am laughed to scorn by him.
Silence, then love. Silence. It's time to strike.
I give my word, and I shall stick to it.

Since this deluding hope embitters me,
Let gentleness give way to hate. It's time
For it in turn to reign within my heart,
And outraged love should cease to act like love.

Scene Seven

MATAMORE

They're coming. Let's escape. There's nobody.
Let's advance boldly. How I'm shivering.
I hear them. Flee. No, it was just the wind.
Let's take advantage of the shades of night.
Despite her father, I'll await my queen.
This band of servants really worries me.
For centuries I've never trembled so.
This is too risky. If they come, I'm dead,
For I would rather die than take them on
And soil my arm in battle with this scum.
What dangers courage can involve one in!
In any case, I'm fleet. If all I need
Is to be fast, I can outsmart them all.
My foot's at least as rapid as my sword.
This time they're here. All's over. I must die.
My body's ice. I'm frozen to the spot.
How adverse to my valour are the fates ...
It's my belovéd with my adjutant.
My body is de-iced. Let's overhear,
And see how skilfully he pleads my case.

Scene Eight

CLINDOR, ISABELLE, MATAMORE

ISABELLE

(*Matamore listens from his hiding-place.*)
All's shaping badly on my father's part.
I've never seen a man so adamant.
He wants neither your master nor yourself.
What's more, your rival has turned jealous, and
This is why I have brought you down below;
They might surprise us in my boudoir. Here
We can converse in full security,
For you can slip away on either side,
And my retreat is clear if someone comes.

CLINDOR

You're too concerned about protecting me.

ISABELLE

I cannot be too much concerned to win
A prize without which all the rest is nought,
Something I value more than all the world,
The reason why I'm glad to be alive.
A rival through my father seeks my hand,
But you alone possess a claim to me.
I'm persecuted by the two of them,
But for your sake I'll gladly suffer all.
And I shall bless these cruel buffetings
If they're endured from faithfulness to you.

CLINDOR

I'm covered with embarrassment. My soul
Can offer in return nought but my life;
My blood is the one thing that's left to me,
Too happy if I lose it serving you!
But if my star should one day brighter shine

And let me see again my native town,
You'll find your choice is not beneath you, that
I'm equal to my rival, all in all.
And yet, despite your loving words, I fear
Father and rival may impose their will.

ISABELLE

Dismiss such fears. Any attempt will fail.
One has less power than the other charm.
I will not say what I'm resolved upon.
I need but stay absolute mistress of
Myself. Then all these plans are vacuous.
Thus . . .

MATAMORE

I can bear no more. I must speak out.

ISABELLE

God! Someone's listening.

CLINDOR

It's our Matamore.
I'll go and calm him down. Don't be alarmed.

Scene Nine

MATAMORE, CLINDOR

MATAMORE

Ah! villain.

CLINDOR

Softly, for these serving-men . . .

MATAMORE

Well, what?

CLINDOR

Will fall upon us presently.

MATAMORE

(*Draws him to a corner of the stage.*)
Come here. You know your crime. To my beloved
You did not speak for *me*, but for yourself.

CLINDOR

Yes, I *did* make a bid for happiness.

MATAMORE

You have the choice between four kinds of death.
I'll smash you with a hammer blow, like glass,
Or thrust you living to the earth's far core,
Make mincemeat of you with a backward stroke,
Throw you so high above the lightning's glare,
You'll be consumed by elemental fire.
Choose promptly then, and settle your affairs.

CLINDOR

You choose yourself.

MATAMORE

What choice do you propose?

CLINDOR

Fly with dispatch or be right soundly thrashed.

MATAMORE

You threaten me again. The cheek of it!
Instead of falling on your knees to me! ...
He's given the signal. Here the servants come ...
I'm off to bid the seas to swallow you.

CLINDOR

You need not seek so large a cemetery.
I'm going, here and now, to throw you in
The river.

MATAMORE

Zounds! They are in league!

CLINDOR

Sing small.
I have already slain ten men tonight;
You'll swell their numbers if you rouse my wrath.

MATAMORE

God's wounds! This rascal blossomed in my shade,
And learned of valour following in my steps.
If he respected me, I'd honour him.
Here. I'm good-hearted. It would never do
To rob the world of such a valiant man;
Implore my pardon and profane no more
By your addresses her whom I adore.
You know my valour. Learn my clemency.

CLINDOR

Rather, if your devotion is so strong,
Let us cross swords for who shall win the prize.

MATAMORE

Your spirited proposal warms my heart.
For such a conquest use no artifice;
I give her to you as your due reward;
Now don't complain of my ingratitude!

CLINDOR

At this rare present, joy is unconfined.
Great kings' protector, generous warrior,
May the whole universe ring with your praise.

Scene Ten

ISABELLE, MATAMORE, CLINDOR

ISABELLE

I thank the heavens for having in the end
Let you, without a fight, become good friends.

MATAMORE

Forget, my queen, the honour that my love
Had thought to do you, taking you to wife.
For various reasons, I have changed my plans,
But I will give you someone of my choice.
Esteem him. He is valiant, too. He fought
Under me.

ISABELLE

Just to please you, I'll accept.

CLINDOR

But we need silence to enjoy our love.

MATAMORE

You shall have silence and protection. Use
My name in all four corners of the world.
I am feared equally on land and sea.
Go and live happily, in marriage bonds.

ISABELLE

The better to obey, I pledge my troth.

CLINDOR

Bid her confirm this troth by giving me . . .

Scene Eleven

GÉRONTE, ADRASTE, MATAMORE, CLINDOR, ISABELLE, LYSE, TROOP OF SERVANTS

ADRASTE

This insolence will cost, suborning knave,
Your life.

MATAMORE

They've caught my courage napping, but
This door is open. Quick. Let's skip upstairs.

(*He goes into Isabelle's room after she and Lyse have entered it.*)

CLINDOR

Villain! You had to use a bandit troop;
But I will pick you out among them all.

(*He runs Adraste through.*)

GÉRONTE

Adraste is wounded! Fetch a doctor. Run.
The rest of you, arrest the murderer.

CLINDOR

I yield to numbers. Farewell, Isabelle.
I fall into a pit my fate has dug.

GÉRONTE

All's over now. Transport this body home.
And you, lead off the victim to the gaol.

Scene Twelve

ALCANDRE, PRIDAMANT

PRIDAMANT

Alas, my son is dead.

ALCANDRE

Be not alarmed!

PRIDAMANT

Refuse him not assistance from your spells.

ALCANDRE

Be patient, and, even without such aid,
You'll see him presently happy in love.

ACT FOUR

Scene One

ISABELLE

Alas! The end is near. An unfair judge
Tomorrow tyrannously immolates
My lover to his would-be murderer,
Meting out vengeance and not punishment.
Tomorrow, by a harsh, unjust decree,
Will see the triumph of a father's hate,
Of local backing and the dead man's rank,
Of my dire misfortune and a cruel fate.
Alas! How many foes, how powerful,
Pitted against the feeble innocence
Of an obscure outsider, whose one fault
Is to have loved me and deserved my love.
Clindor, your virtues and your honest suit
Both won my heart and constitute your crime.
But, though I could live on when you are dead,
I mean to lose my life on losing you;
When they pronounce your doom, they sentence *me*.
I follow you in death since I'm its cause.
And our two deaths coincident will be
With our reunion in the life to come.
Thus to your disappointment you will see,
Father, the happy outcome of our love;
And, if my death should plunge you in despair,
Beside my lover, I will mock your tears.
Any remorse you feel or tears you shed
Will but enhance our mutual delight.
Or, if that's not sufficient torture, then
My shade will every day curdle your blood,
Dogging your footsteps in the ghastly dark,

Unfold to you a thousand gloomy scenes,
Pursue you with perpetual fears, reproach
You with my death and call you after me,
Pour on your ebbing life torrential woe,
And force you finally to envy me.

Scene Two

ISABELLE, LYSE

LYSE

What! Everyone's asleep, and you are up?
I swear to you your father's much concerned.

ISABELLE

When hope is dying, fear can not survive.
I find relief in giving vent to tears.
For the last time here I beheld Clindor;
This spot best echoed his melodious voice,
And to my mind distraught brings back again
Vividly his endearing memory.

LYSE

How busily you swell your sufferings.

ISABELLE

What would you have me do in my despair?

LYSE

Two perfect suitors sought your hand. Of these
One must tomorrow die; the other's dead.
Waste not your time in mourning them, but try
To find another worth the pair of them.

ISABELLE

How dare you make suggestions such as these?

LYSE

What do you hope for from misguided grief?
Think you by weeping, tarnishing your charms,
Back from the gates of death to call Clindor?
You should be rather planning conquests new.
I know of someone interested in you,
A man beyond compare.

ISABELLE

Begone from here.

LYSE

The best of minds could make no better choice.

ISABELLE

Must I look on while you increase my woe?

LYSE

Must I disguise from you the joy I feel?

ISABELLE

Whence comes this most unreasonable joy?

LYSE

When I have told you, judge if I am right.

ISABELLE

Ah, tell me nothing.

LYSE

This concerns you, though.

ISABELLE

Talk only of Clindor, or hold your tongue.

LYSE

My happy nature, smiling even in storms,
Can do more in a trice than floods of tears
For it. It has saved Clindor.

ISABELLE

Clindor?

LYSE

Why, yes.

ISABELLE

Judge after that of my devotion.

LYSE

Ah?

ISABELLE

I beg you. Tell me where I'll find him, Lyse.

LYSE

I've but begun. You must take over now.

ISABELLE

Ah! Lyse.

LYSE

But would you really follow him?

ISABELLE

Follow the man I cannot live without?
If you can not release him from his bonds,
I'll go with him down to the deepest hell.
Come. Ask no more if I would follow him.

LYSE

Since love has brought you to this pretty pass,
Listen how far I've got. Further my plans.

You'll be alone to blame if he's not saved.
The prison is near by.

ISABELLE

And so?

LYSE

Each day
The keeper's brother catches sight of me
And, since to see me is to love me, he,
Poor fellow, has succumbed to my allures.

ISABELLE

I never knew of this.

LYSE

I was ashamed.
I died of fear lest you were told of it.
But, since Clindor's arrest four days ago,
I've lent my suitor a more willing ear,
And, pandering to his hopes with eyes and lips,
I have pretended to respond to him.
When a man thinks his passion is returned,
He will do anything for his adored.
Thus I've made sure I have him in my hand,
And he will never dare to say me nay.
When he no longer doubted he was loved,
I turned him down on occupation's grounds.
He to oblige me swore he hated it,
But said he could not change it easily.
The prison keys, entrusted to his charge,
Were his main income and his brother's. I
Told him immediately his lucky star
Could not provide a better chance than this
To make his fortune and to win my hand.
He only had to make the most of it.
He held in bonds a lord of Brittany
Disguised under the name of Delamont.

The prisoner must be saved, escorted home;
Then he could always have a patron's help.
He was amazed. I pressed him. He declined.
He spoke of love to me, and I refused.
I left him angrily. He followed me
Abashed, apologized, and I again
Refused.

ISABELLE

And in the end?

LYSE

When I went back,
He wavered. I attacked, but he held out.
This morning, 'In a word,' I said to him,
'The danger's pressing, but you can do all.
Your brother's absent.' 'But,' he said, 'we need
Some money to prepare for such a trip.
The gentleman has none.'

ISABELLE

Ah, Lyse, at once
You should have offered everything we had –
Pearls, rings and clothes.

LYSE

In fact, I did much more.
I said the prisoner did you fealty,
That you who loved him too would flee with us.
This made him most accommodating, and
I realized a touch of jealousy
Of Clindor had confused his reasoning,
That all his hesitations had been caused
By idle fears that we were sweethearts. For
He left as soon as he was undeceived.
The way was clear. He guaranteed success.
He told me to transmit this message. Be
Prepared, when midnight strikes, to steal away.

ISABELLE

How happy, thanks to you . . .

LYSE

Add to all this
That, by accepting someone I dislike,
I sacrifice myself for your content.

ISABELLE

For this . . .

LYSE

I need no thanks from you. Be off,
And do your packing, and, to swell the sum,
Add to your jewels all the old man's crowns.
I'm selling you his treasures on the cheap;
I stole his keys after he went to bed.
Take them.

ISABELLE

Let's do the job together.

LYSE

No.
Do it without my help.

ISABELLE

What! You're afraid?

LYSE

No, but it's guaranteed to wake him up.
We'd never keep ourselves from chattering.

ISABELLE

You madcap.

LYSE

But, for fear of being caught,
I must await the leader here. He would,
Loitering in the street, be recognized.
Let's contact him as soon as he arrives.
This is, upon my word . . .

ISABELLE

Goodbye, I'm off.
I'll let you act the mistress for today.

LYSE

At least . . .

ISABELLE

Be sure to watch.

LYSE

And you to loot.

Scene Three

LYSE

Thus, Clindor, I alone decide your fate.
I free you from the chains I put you in,
And *I* at will can make you live or die.
Vengeance was mine beyond my wildest dreams;
It was to check your pleasures that I schemed,
But your harsh sentence made me change my mind.
Now I would save your pleasures and your life;
And love for you, when danger threatens you,
Revives and warns me I have gone too far.
I hope then, Clindor, that your gratitude
Stifling your roving and ungrateful love . . .

Scene Four

MATAMORE, ISABELLE, LYSE

ISABELLE

What, here at night!

MATAMORE

The other day . . .

ISABELLE

What's this?
'The other day', and still I find you here!

LYSE

It's Matamore. Why, where did he get caught?

ISABELLE

As I went up the staircase, he came down.

MATAMORE

The other day, as next best thing to love,
I guaranteed you my protection.

ISABELLE

Well,
And then?

MATAMORE

They started up a rough-house here.
You went in, seeing this skullduggery.
I, to protect you, followed you at once.

ISABELLE

Your valour had a generous intent?
Later?

MATAMORE

To guard someone so beautiful,
I then stood sentry on the highest floor.

ISABELLE

And never left it.

MATAMORE

No.

LYSE

In language plain,
Terror confined him to the lumber room.

MATAMORE

Terror?

LYSE

You tremble. Yours is *sans pareil.*

MATAMORE

I made it my Bucephalus[1], because
It's a good mount. I broke it, trembling, in;
And, since then, when I move, it trembles still.

LYSE

You show a rare caprice in choosing mounts.

MATAMORE

To haste to great adventures speedily.

ISABELLE

You make it sound impressive, but let's change
The subject. You were there four days?

1. The favourite horse of Alexander the Great.

MATAMORE

I was.

LYSE

And lived?

MATAMORE

On nectar and ambrosia.

LYSE

One easily gets sated with such food.

MATAMORE

By no means.

ISABELLE

In the end, you did come down . . .

MATAMORE

To give you back your love into your arms,
To throw his prison open, smash its gates,
And break to smithereens his stoutest chains.

LYSE

Be frank. Confess that, urged by hunger's pangs,
To raid the bread bin was your real intent.

MATAMORE

Both of them. This ambrosia's poor fare.
It turned my stomach after just one day.
A dainty dish, but won't sustain a man.
Only a god can thrive on such a food.
It's bad for one. A single mouthful makes
The teeth grow longer and the body shrink.

LYSE

In short, it's fine, but not your cup of tea!

MATAMORE

And hence, each night I took a turn downstairs,
And there, just making do with kitchen scraps
I mingled human viands with divine.

ISABELLE

So after all you had intent to steal.

MATAMORE

You yourselves after all dare slander me?
If I should ever let my choler rise . . .

ISABELLE

Lyse, call me out my father's serving-men.

MATAMORE

You think I'm waiting.

Scene Five

ISABELLE, LYSE

LYSE

There's no holding him.

ISABELLE

He told us what a rapid steed was fear!

LYSE

But meantime naught or little has been done.

ISABELLE

Nothing at all, but he's to blame for that.

LYSE

But all you had to do was let him go.

ISABELLE

He recognized me and accosted me.
Alone at night, I feared his insolence,
And even more lest he should make a scene.
Just to get rid of him and be relieved,
The best course seemed to me to bring him here.
See, when I have your help, how brave I am,
Since I dare face this violent character.

LYSE

I laughed like you, but I protested. What
A waste of time!

ISABELLE

I shall make up for it.

LYSE

This is the master-mind who hatched our plot.
Hear first of all how great his zeal has been.

Scene Six

ISABELLE, LYSE, THE GAOLER

ISABELLE

Well! my good friend, shall we defy the fates?
Do you come here to bring me life or death?
In you alone we place our fondest hopes.

THE GAOLER

Banish your fears. Everything's going well.
We can leave now. My horses are prepared.
Soon you can laugh at dangers of arrest.

ISABELLE

A guardian angel you shall be for us.
I never can reward you fittingly.

THE GAOLER (*pointing to Lyse*)

This is the sole reward my heart demands.

ISABELLE

You must resolve to make him satisfied.

LYSE

But all his preparations are in vain.
How can we open wide the city's gates?

THE GAOLER

Horses are ready in the suburbs, and
I know a stretch of wall that's falling down
At which it will be easy to get out.

ISABELLE

I am on tenterhooks.

THE GAOLER

We must make haste.

ISABELLE

Agreed. And we shall leave immediately.
Come on upstairs and help me raid the till.

Scene Seven

CLINDOR (*in prison*)

Sweet recollections of my dear delight,
Which soon will change to execution. How,
Despite the horrors of this mortal fear,
Your murmurs echo gently in my ear.
Do not abandon me. Abide by me
More than the rigours of a cruel fate,
And, when the darkest hues of death depict
The dire misfortunes now in store for me,
Depict as well to my dejected soul

My fortune, far beyond what I deserved.
When I complain of their severity,
Remind me how exceeding rash I was;
That my low status for such lofty aims
Made my hopes guilty and my love unjust;
That I, as suitor, was a criminal,
And that my death is a just punishment.
Yet, in the end, I have this happiness –
I die, fair Isabelle, for serving you,
And, even if the sword descends on me,
I die too glorious since I die for you.
Alas! How I delude myself, for nought
Can hide from me the gallows' infamy.
What greater suffering than to leave these eyes
Whose fatal love makes me so glorious?
The shadow of a murderer dogs my steps,
Alive, he perished; dead, he murders me.
His name undoes me when his arm could not.
A thousand murderers spring from his death;
And from his blood, fertile in perfidy,
Arise against me men unscrupulous
Whose passions, masked by cold authority,
Can do state murder with impunity.
Tomorrow, courage will be shown as crime
And my head offered to a treacherous knave.
The public voice so strongly speaks for him,
The trial's outcome hardly is in doubt.
Thus from all sides my downfall was assured.
I fought back death; this is the penalty.
One peril I avoided, but I pass
From rival's hand to executioner's.
I shudder when I think of my mishaps;
Even in rest I am upon the rack;
At dead of night, when sleep descends on all,
I see the shameful instrument of death;
I have before my eyes the hangman's face;
From the tribunal, sentence is pronounced;
I leave the court with fetters on my feet;

I hear the insolent crowds that follow me;
I see the preparation for my death;
There my mind falters, and my reason whirls.
I can see naught that promises me aid;
And fear of death already makes me die.
Isabelle, you alone, by thoughts of love,
You dissipate these terrors, calm my soul,
And, when I call to mind your heavenly charms,
These sordid visions vanish from my sight.
However harsh adversity's assaults,
Remember me. I'll think I live again.

(*He hears a noise*)

How comes it that at night my prison door
Opens. What make you here at such a time?

Scene Eight

CLINDOR, THE GAOLER

THE GAOLER (*while Isabelle and Lyse are seen in the offing*)

The judges meeting to decide your case,
Moved by compassion, have relented.

CLINDOR

God!
Relented!

THE GAOLER

Yes. For you will die at night.

CLINDOR

Is that as far as their compassion goes?

THE GAOLER

How lightly you esteem this clemency;
You're saved the shame of public hanging.

CLINDOR

Well,
What incense can I offer to the men
Who now relent, but send me to my death?

THE GAOLER

You should receive the news with better grace.

CLINDOR

Come, do your duty, friend, and hold your tongue.

THE GAOLER

A band of archers waits for you without;
You may feel better when you see their face.

Scene Nine

CLINDOR, ISABELLE, LYSE, THE GAOLER

ISABELLE (*speaking to Lyse, while the gaoler opens the prison to Clindor*)

We soon shall see him, Lyse.

LYSE

What joy for you!

ISABELLE

Should I not laugh when I'm restored to life?
His fate and mine run parallel, and I
Would die of the same blow that spelt his end!

THE GAOLER

Do you know many archers, Sir, like this?

CLINDOR

Ah, Isabelle, it's you! What a surprise!
(*To the gaoler*)
Kindly deceiver, you were right to say
That I would die at night, but of content.

ISABELLE

Clindor!

THE GAOLER

There's no time for endearments, friends.
Later we'll see to our fiancées.

CLINDOR

What!
Lyse your fiancée?

ISABELLE

Listen to the tale
Of how you owe your freedom to their love.

THE GAOLER

When we are safely hid, we can relax,
But now our aim is to escape arrest.

ISABELLE

Let's flee, but first promise me both of you
Until your marriage to restrain yourselves.
Otherwise . . .

CLINDOR

If that's all that worries you,
I promise you I will.

THE GAOLER

And so do I.

ISABELLE

With such a noble pledge, I dare risk all.

THE GAOLER

No more delay. Quick! Let's get out of here.

Scene Ten

ALCANDRE, PRIDAMANT

ALCANDRE

No longer fear peril or death for them.
Many will look for them, but find no trace.

PRIDAMANT

At last I breathe.

ALCANDRE

After this stroke of luck,
Two years have raised them to high honours. You
Will not be shown their travels or be told
Whether they found calm waters or survived,
Or by what art they rose to fame. For you,
All you need see is how they saved themselves,
And, without boring you with lengthy tales,
I'll show them at the height of fortune. But,
Since we must now pass on to grander things,
Let's conjure up new phantoms. Those you saw
Were representing in succession, Sir,
Their[1] love and flight to your astounded eyes.
But, as they[1] were not called to high estate,
We need another and more splendid set!

1. The characters.

ACT FIVE

Scene One

ALCANDRE, PRIDAMANT

PRIDAMANT

How changed is Isabelle! How glamorous!

ALCANDRE

Lyse is beside her acting as her maid.
But once again, above all, have no fear,
And leave this spot only when I have gone.
I stress the point again. Your life's at stake.

PRIDAMANT

Your warning weakens any such desire.

Scene Two

ISABELLE (*in the part of Hippolyta*), LYSE (*in the part of Clarina*)

LYSE

This walk you're taking, will it never end?
And will you pass the night here in these grounds?

ISABELLE

I cannot hide the reason I am here;
Silence would but increase my suffering.
Prince Florilame . . .

LYSE

Well, he is absent now.

ISABELLE

That is the source of all my present ills;
We are his neighbours. He is fond of us,
And lets us use the door into his grounds.
Princess Rosine and my perfidious spouse,
While he is absent, have appointments here.
I shall accost him and shall let him know
I'll not put up with infidelity.

LYSE

Lady, believe me, do not tax him home.
You would do better to dissimulate.
We profit little from such jealous scenes;
They make a man persist in his affairs.
He's always master; anything we say
Will in the end recoil against us.

ISABELLE

What!
Should I then overlook adultery?
Another has his heart, I but the name.
Can he unblemished break his marriage troth?
Does he not blush at infidelity?

LYSE

That was so once upon a time, but now
Marriage and faithfulness cut little ice.
Their reputation has its special rules.
Our good name may be lost. *Theirs* runs no risk;
It's aided by our craven weaknesses;
The honour of a man's to have affairs.

ISABELLE

Dismiss this honour and this vanity
Which earns repute by sheer unfaithfulness.

If to hate change and have no lady love
For such a man's to curry infamy,
I feel such vileness should be gloried in.
If he's despised for that, long live such scorn.
The fault of loving one's own wife too much
For virtuous husbands is a splendid fault!

LYSE

He's just come in. I hear the door swing to.

ISABELLE

Let's flee.

LYSE

He's seen you and is following you.

Scene Three

CLINDOR (*in the part of Theagenes*), ISABELLE (*in the part of Hippolyta*), and LYSE (*in the part of Clarina*)

CLINDOR

You flee, my dear, and seek to put me off.
Are these the sweets of love you promised me?
Is this how lovers should conduct a tryst?
Flee not, my dearest one, and have no fear.
Florilame is away. My wife's asleep.

ISABELLE

But are you sure she is?

CLINDOR

Ah, hostile fate!

ISABELLE

I am awake and am no longer blind;
Even in the night I see only too clear;

I see all my suspicions justified,
And cannot doubt your base ingratitude.
By your own mouth your secret is betrayed.
O careful lover, what farsightedness!
And how extremely wise it is in love
Completely to confide in your own wife!
Where are your vows to honour none but me?
What have you done, then, with your heart, your troth?
When I received it, ingrate, you recall
How much your fortunes differed from my own,
How many rivals' proffers I disdained,
You but a humble soldier, they great lords;
What tender love my father wrapped me in!
I left it, though, to share your poverty.
I gladly was abducted. Thus I foiled
His plan to make me bow to his command.
Since then to what extremity was I
Reduced by all the hazards of your flight?
And what did I not suffer till good luck
Raised you from your estate to this high rank?
If you give up your troth for happiness,
Restore me to the home you tore from me.
The love I bore you made me hazard all,
Not to win greatness but a life with you.

CLINDOR

Tax me not with your passion and your flight.
What does not love do when it rules the soul?
Since you were subjugated by its power,
Not *me* you followed but your own desires,
Then I was nobody; but *now* recall
Your flight made both our fortunes equal and,
If I abducted you, I was not moved
By your great wealth which did not come with you.
I had to back me nothing but my sword,
And you contributed your love alone.
Thanks to that sword, I rose to greatness here.
Your love spelt for me dangers infinite.

But now you miss your father and your wealth,
Resent consorting with princesses. Then
Return back home and let your riches earn
The honours given you by your present rank.
What grounds have you to be dissatisfied?
When have I ever sought to use constraint?
Have you been treated coldly or despised?
Women have strange ideas, I must say!
A husband may adore them and submit
With boundless love to their bizarre demands;
He may heap honours on them, kindnesses,
And leave no stone unturned to pleasure them.
Yet, if he stray from virtue but an inch,
For *them* there is no crime so serious.
It's theft, perfidiousness, murder, poisoning,
Cutting a father's throat, burning the home.
Of old, the Titans' fearful punishment
Fell with less justice on Encelades.[1]

ISABELLE

As I have said, I never was concerned
With rank and station. It was only you
I followed when I left my father's house;
But, since success has turned your head, forget
That I'm involved. Think whom you owe it to –
To Florilame alone. He raised you from
Obscurity as soon as you appeared.
You rose from soldier to commander, and
The rare good luck of this appointment soon
Attracted you the favours of the king.
What active friendship has he not deployed
To cultivate the harvest he had sown?
Thanks to his growing efforts, are you not
A little less in rank but more in power?
It would have won even the most savage heart.
Yet you, as thanks, would seek to stain his couch.

1. One of the fifty-headed giants who made war on the gods.

Find some excuses for your brutishness.
His benefactions brand your treachery.
You take his favours, yet you steal his wife.
He made of you a lord. You smirch his name,
Ingrate, who thus returns evil for good.
This is how you display your gratitude.

CLINDOR

My soul (for still this fairest name is yours,
And will be yours until the day I die),
Think you respect for him or fear of death
Can ever wrest me from what *you* can not?
Say I am ingrate. Call me quite forsworn.
But do not wrong our sacred passion. *That*
Is still as vigorous as once it was,
And if this passion that has conquered me
Could have been stifled at its birth, the love
I bear you would have had the power then;
Honour in vain endeavours to resist;
You yourself know it cannot be subdued.
This god who forced you to abandon home,
Country and wealth to follow poverty,
This same god now compels me inwardly
To rob you of a trifling sigh or two.
Allow some latitude to waywardness
And have no fears your place will be usurped.
The love that does not rest on virtue's rock
Destroys itself and passes in a flash;
But that which joins us is more firmly based;
There honour shines, there virtue still presides;
It gathers new attractions as it goes.
And its firm bonds last until death divides.
My soul, yet once again, pardon the trick
This tyrant of the heart has played on me;
Suffer an insane passion of a day
Which does not undermine our married love.

ISABELLE

Alas! how fondly I delude myself!
Deceived, I yet convince myself I'm loved;
Lulled by endearing words, I can excuse
A crime because I love the criminal.
Forgive, dear husband, my poor self-control.
I let my feelings carry me away.
I would in such a tempest lack a heart
If I looked on unmoved and undismayed.
Since beauty passes and complexions fade,
It's natural your love should also flag;
This passing fancy, I can even believe,
Will alter nothing in our married love.
But think who is the lady you desire,
What danger her position spells for you.
Dissimulate, mislead and be discreet.
The great, in love, never know secrecy;
The hangers-on whom they attract in swarms
Are, Argus-like, all eyes that naught escapes,
And there's not one of them that would not try
To curry favour by malicious tales.
Sooner or later Florilame will learn,
Either from his mistrust or from his men.
And then (I shudder at the very thought),
To what extremes will not his fury go!
Since to these pastimes you are so inclined,
Pursue your pleasures, but be on your guard.
I would impassive see you faithless if
You ran no danger from your faithlessness.

CLINDOR

Lady, must I again repeat to you
My life is nought to me compared with love?
My heart in love is stricken far too sore
To fear the perils I am threatened by.
My passion blinds me, and for such a prize
I hazard little hazarding my head.

My passion time alone can moderate;
It's a torrential force that cannot last.

ISABELLE

Well, hasten to the death that beckons you;
Be careless of your life as of my tears.
Think you this prince, after so base a crime,
Will by your punishment be satisfied?
Whom can I look to when your sordid death
To his just vengeance will expose his wife,
And, on the spouse of a false foreigner,
He seeks to wreak revenge a second time?
No. I'll not wait until your certain end
Brings down on me your second punishment,
And seeks my honour, guarded jealously,
To immolate to his resentment. No.
I will forestall the shame you bring on me
And die if you refuse to opt for life.
This body which in love I gave to you
Will soon not fear a ravisher's attack.
I've lived for love, not for the infamy
Of serving your illustrious mistress' spouse.
Farewell. Dying before you, at the least
I'll mitigate your crime and set you free.

CLINDOR

Die not, but by a second change of heart
Behold the marvel of your virtue's power.
To love me faithless and by suicide
To help ward off a base attack on me!
I do not know which I should most admire,
Your boundless courage or your boundless love;
Both overwhelm me. I am yours again.
Lady, my brutish ardour is at bay.
All's over. It is dead. My soul, reformed,
Lady, has sundered its degrading chains.
My heart, captured, put up a poor defence;
Cancel the memory.

ISABELLE

It's quite forgot.

CLINDOR

Let all the fairest women in the world
Conspire henceforward to lay siege to me;
This heart, impregnable to their assaults,
Will have, as gods and masters, but your eyes.

LYSE

Someone is coming.

Scene Four

CLINDOR (*in the part of Theagenes*), ISABELLE (*in the part of Hippolyta*), LYSE (*in the part of Clarina*), ERASTE, TROOP OF FLORILAME'S SERVANTS.

ERASTE (*stabbing Clindor*)

Knave, receive with joy
The favours your belovéd sends to you.

PRIDAMANT (*to Alcandre*)

He's being murdered. Gods, I beg you, help.

ERASTE

May all suborners always perish thus!

ISABELLE

What have you done?

ERASTE

A great and righteous deed
Which with affright will chill posterity,
In order to teach ingrates, by his blood,
Never to smirch the honour of a prince.

Our weapons have avenged Lord Florilame,
The outraged princess and yourself. We give
As victim to all three your faithless spouse,
Who was not worthy of your hand and heart.
Accept the punishment for his amours,
And don't complain of justice done to you.
Farewell.

ISABELLE

You've massacred but half of him;
He lives in me. Revel in your revenge.
Finish your work, assassins! Take my life.
Dear husband, they have killed you in my arms,
And even the inner promptings of my heart
Could not by their forebodings save your life.
O clarity, too accurate, too late!
You let us see the evil as it's done.
Should you have . . . But I suffocate. Alas!
My strength, my voice are overborne by grief.
Its sharp excess kills and consoles me both,
Since it unites us . . .

LYSE

She's bereft of speech.
Lady . . . She's dying. Let us save our breath,
And hurry to the house to call for help!

(*At this point, a drop curtain is let down which covers the bodies of Clindor and Isabelle, and the magician and the father leave the cave.*)

Scene Five

ALCANDRE, PRIDAMANT

ALCANDRE

Thus fortune mocks our hopes, and everything
Rises and falls with the revolving wheel,

And its erratic order rules the world,
Causing reverses and not happiness.

PRIDAMANT

This maxim's hardly suited to me, though
It might perhaps assuage a milder grief.
But, having seen my son brutally stabbed,
My pleasures blighted and my hope destroyed,
I would by such disaster be unscathed
If I could think such philosophic thoughts.
Alas, in poverty he did not die;
His death was due to his prosperity.
Do not expect further laments from me.
Grief that laments seeks to be comforted,
But mine goes to its pitiable fate.
Farewell. I'll die since now my son is dead.

ALCANDRE

This outburst of despair is natural,
And to divert it would be criminal.
To follow your dear son you need not wait,
But spare yourself this suicidal act.
Give free scope to the grief that gnaws your heart,
And, to increase it, see his funeral.

(*Here, the curtain is raised, and all the actors appear with their door-keeper. They are counting out money on a table, and each is taking his share.*)

PRIDAMANT

What's this? They count out cash among the dead?

ALCANDRE

Don't they! Why, none of them will miss a sou.

PRIDAMANT

But it's Clindor. O God! what a surprise!
I see his murderers, his wife and Lyse.

What spell has sudden stifled their disputes,
Thus to unite the living and the dead?

ALCANDRE

These are the members of an actors' troop
Who share their takings based upon their parts.
One kills, one dies, one causes tears to flow,
But it's the stage that shapes their enmity.
They fight in verse. Death follows on their words.
Dropping the borrowed passions of their roles,
The traitor, the betrayed, the live, the dead,
Are, when the curtain falls, friends as before.
Your son and followers managed to flee
And shake her father off and the police,
But, straitened circumstances compelling them,
Decided on the stage as a career.

PRIDAMANT

My son an actor!

ALCANDRE

Of this complex art
All four have made a haven from distress;
And, since his prison days, what you have seen –
His errant love, his unforeseen demise –
Is the dénouement of a tragic play,
Which he presents today upon the stage,
Wherein his colleagues in this noble craft
Delight all Paris and its citizens.
They keep their earnings. This rich costumr'y
I showed you in its full magnificence
It is Clindor's, but it is only used
When on the stage he reaps the pit's applause.

PRIDAMANT

I thought his death was real; it was but feigned;
Yet I find everywhere grounds for lament.

Is this the glory, this the honoured rank,
To which good fortune was to help him rise?

ALCANDRE

Cease to lament at it. The theatre
Is at so high a point, all worship it;
And what your age regarded with contempt
Is now the darling of all men of taste,
The talk of Paris, and the province's
Desire, the sweet diversion of our kings,
The people's joy, the pleasure of the great;
For it ranks first among their pastimes now,
And those whose splendid statesmanship preserves
By its illustrious measures all the world
Find in the sweetness of so fine a sight
Means to unbend from such exacting tasks.
Even our great King, that thunderbolt of war,
Whose name strikes terror through the universe,
His brow encircled in a laurel crown,
Deigns cast an eye upon the stage of France.
Parnassus there displays its marvels, and
The rarest minds to this devote their nights,
And all of those on whom Apollo smiles
Devote to it some of their learnéd works.
Besides, if standing's rated by one's wealth,
The theatre's a profitable line;
Your son's extracted from this pleasant trade
More affluence than had he stayed at home.
Discard this common error, finally,
And do not mourn for his good fortune.

PRIDAMANT

No,
I dare not now complain. I see how much
His present trade is better than my own.
Admittedly, I was at first alarmed;
I thought the stage was still as once it was.
I criticized it as I did not know

Its spell, its glamour and its usefulness.
But, since your explanations, in my joy
This error and my sadness have been banned.
Clindor has chosen well.

ALCANDRE

See for yourself.

PRIDAMANT

Tomorrow I propose to do just that.
I haste to Paris. But, divine Alcandre,
What can I offer you for what you've done?

ALCANDRE

I only seek to help all men of worth,
And my reward is in your happiness.
Farewell. I'm satisfied since you are so.

PRIDAMANT

Such kindnesses cannot be recompensed.
But, great magician, this at least believe:
They will live ever in my memory.

END

In [illegible]

In South Africa: Please [illegible] Longman Penguin Southern Africa [illegible]

READ MORE IN PENGUIN

READ MORE IN PENGUIN